GUINEA PIG

– Care 101 –

A DEFINITIVE GUIDE

SAURAV

DISCLAIMER

I as an author have made every effort to ensure that the information in this book was correct and updated at the time of release.

The author and publisher do not assume and hereby disclaim any liability to any party for any loss, damage, or disruption caused by errors or omissions, whether such errors or omissions result from negligence, accident, or any other cause.

The authors and publishers advise readers to take full responsibility for the safety of their pets.

The book is intended to help owners understand their pet better. We have discussed about their daily care, diet, health issues and more.

However, this book is not intended as a substitute for the medical advice of veterinarians.

Some guinea pigs might have a different need depending upon their medical condition, breed, and current diet.

The reader should regularly consult a veterinarian in matters relating to the health of his/her pet and particularly with respect to any symptoms that may require diagnosis or medical attention.

The author of this book is neither a veterinarian nor a professional guinea pig breeder. He has shared what he has learned from experience and exposure in the last decade or so living with his guinea pigs.

Please consult a vet immediately if your guinea pig is in any kind of trouble or shows any unusual behavior.

Acknowledgment

Thank you for buying this book! We sincerely hope that this book will be helpful to you in many ways.

In this book, we have tried to provide you with all the information you need to take a good care of your guinea pigs.

The book is well-formatted in an easy to read manner so that even your kids can learn from the book.

All the information presented in the book is shared from the personal experience of the author, and all the data is collected from verified and trusted sources only.

We understand that no guide can be fully complete. However, we have tried to cover as much information as possible.

However, we strongly encourage you to learn more about your guinea pigs from credible sources, talk to other guinea pig owners, and pay a visit to the veterinarian in case of any emergency or medical-related conditions.

TABLE OF CONTENTS

INTRODUCTION

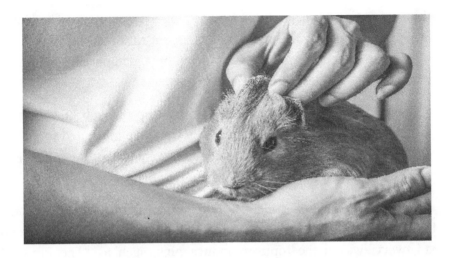

If you want to get a new pet, why not get a guinea pig? They are fun, lovable creatures who make great pets for people of all ages. Like most domestic animals, you can get many different breeds of cavy - But how do you know which one is best for you?

You can get many different types of guinea pigs; they come in shapes, colors, and patterns.

When deciding which cavy breed you wish to get you'll need to decide how much time you will have every day to look after your piggy - this is because some breeds require more care (although all guinea pigs do need a caring owner and all their needs catered for) - long-haired breeds especially need more time spent on them as they need to be groomed thoroughly every day to keep them in prime condition.

One of the first things to establish when looking at guinea pig breeds is to recognize that a lot of breeds come in lots of colors, but also lots of color patterns are not breeds - this means that the dutch pattern is a color and not a breed as you can get many different breeds of guinea pig all with dutch markings.

One way to tell a breed from color is that the breed will often have a coat-type texture that is only associated with that breed, for example, hair in rosettes is nearly always the Abyssinian breed.

In the tradition of recent hits like The Dog Whisperer and The Horse Whisperer, Guinea Pig Definite Guide sets out to unveil the secrets of everything you need to know about Guinea pigs, deciphering them in a way that's easy to understand for an average person.

Guinea Pig Definite Guide goes step by step through all the most important topics that a new owner or even someone interested in guinea pigs needs to know. It does so in a concise, easy-to-read manner filled with full-color photographs and informative charts.

Beginning with a look at the history of guinea pigs and how they came to be introduced to the Western world, the book then moves into several broad overviews on the topic of guinea pigs, such as "The Physical Attributes of Guinea Pig," and "How Many Types of Guinea Pigs Are There?", a chapter that tells you what to expect from a guinea pig, and more importantly, what your guinea pig will expect from you.

Understanding the responsibilities that accompany guinea pig ownership is essential before you commit to bringing one into your home. This book certainly reflects that with its extensive coverage of such an important issue.

It's after this point, though, that Guinea Pig Definite Guide truly comes into its own as a unique offering in guinea pig writings. The book goes fairly in-depth into how to interpret the signs a guinea pig gives you and how you should respond. For instance, it tells you how different pairings of guinea pig sexes will get along with one another if introduced into the same environment.

It tells you what to do (and what NOT to do) if your guinea pig happens to get outside and runs away. Also included is a chart indicating the dozens of different sounds and postures that a guinea pig is capable of displaying, as well as an exhaustive look inside the animal's head that lets us know how to interpret these signs for what they are. The highlight of the chapters, however, might be the extensive advice given on behavioral conditioning.

Though guinea pigs are typically sweet, mild-mannered creatures, there are some instances in which they can bite or otherwise act in an undesirable manner. Guinea Pig Definite Guide shows how to handle each of these cases to effectively address the unmet concerns of the guinea pig and help return him or her to their natural, agreeable state of mind.

Guinea Pig Definite Guide covers a massive amount of material with extensive looks at the different types of food available for your guinea pig and which of those he or she is likely to find the most preferable. Topics also include the specific nutritional needs of the guinea pig, such as the minimum levels of Vitamin C and calcium that should be maintained for proper health.

These figures are handily cross-referenced in an easy-to-read chart that tells you at a glance what adjustments you might need to make in the diet of your guinea pig if he or she doesn't seem to be operating at full capacity.

The most important chapter in the book is a compendium of guinea pig health and hygiene information, including such in-depth topics as how to best design a guinea pig's habitat to suit their climate needs (which can be different depending on the length of the animal's coat).

Grooming is given a lot of coverage, and not just for regular activities like brushing and bathing, but also how to inspect your guinea pig's teeth for damage or infections, as well as the deceptively complex task of trimming their toenails.

Special care is given to a broad section on symptoms that an ailing guinea pig might display and what particular disease or problem those symptoms are indicative of. The controversy of guinea pig antibiotics is given a lot of consideration and gives you enough information to make the right decision where this is concerned. Should the time come that you need to do so?

Lastly, a properly stocked "guinea pig medicine cabinet" is invaluable information that every owner should know.

The amount of information covered in Guinea Pig Definite Guide is probably so extensive that it touches upon things you would never have thought to ask otherwise.

The goal of this guide is to allow you to have a happy and enjoyable relationship with your guinea pig and to ensure that they never come to be in the same sad situation that caused them to be with us here at the awl in the first place.

CHAPTER 1

PHYSICAL OVERVIEW OF A GUINEA PIG

INTRO ON HOW A HEALTHY GUINEA PIG LOOK

Good physical characteristics. By looking at the overall condition of the guinea pig's body. The guinea pig should be neither fat nor thin, with no swelling, lumps, or bumps. The guinea pigs coat should be well-groomed, without bare patches (full, soft, and smooth looking). By all means possible, avoid guinea pigs with bald patches or red patches skin.

Guinea Pigs are genuinely sociable creatures. They love each other's company, so they must have at least another guinea pig to interact within their lives. The best guinea pig groupings are either two males together or two or more females. You can also add one neutered male with a herd of females; that way, the male keeps the peace among the girls, so you don't get any unintended baby guinea pigs.

While more than two males can live together in harmony, you're taking a big risk because they're more likely to fight, and you might find yourself having to make the heartbreaking decision to separate them. The Male guinea pigs are known as boars, females' guinea pigs are called sows, and the baby guinea pigs are known as pups.

WEIGHT

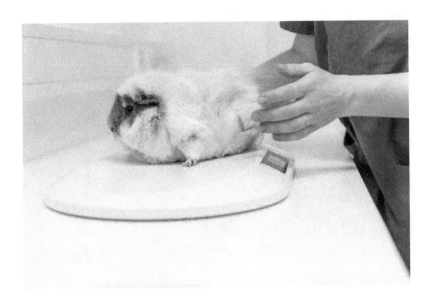

This can be difficult because of the normal body shape of a guinea pig. Some guinea pigs are also just bigger than others. According to the book "Ferrets, Rabbits, and Rodents Clinical Medicine and Surgery," Guinea pig weights can vary from 900 to 1,200 grams for males and 700 to 900 grams for females.

The weight of your guinea pig is one of its most important health and wellbeing indicators. As such, you must track and monitor your pets' weight over time, see how they naturally grow and be able to detect any unexpected changes early, and respond quickly. The following guide describes what, at different ages, is considered a 'normal' guinea pig weight, and also describes how to measure it.

Fast, significant weight loss – or gain in weight – will always be a cause of concern. Handling alone doesn't always allow you to catch up on the beginnings of any weight changes. Guinea pigs are prey animals and are very good at 'hiding' a disease. That's why keeping a record is vital, and getting to know the 'norm' for your piggies is.

Size

Guinea pigs are somewhat unusual among pet rodents because they grow much larger than their furry relatives, including mice, rats, and hamsters. What's a 'typical' or 'average' size for a guinea pig, then? The following statistics will provide you with a rough understanding of how long your cavy will be in different life stages.

Birth

A guinea pig at birth is typically about 8-10 cm (3-4 inches) in length. You should expect a normal difference in size in a litter between the animals, with some larger than others. Often, the number of pups in the litter determines how large each baby is a larger litter appears to produce smaller offspring.

This makes sense because the more babies inside the sow, the less space they have to develop. Litter sizes tend to vary from 1 to 6 pups, but a litter of 2 to 4 is more common.

Growth

Guinea pigs grow very quickly, and after just eight weeks, they can double in size to around 15-20 cm (6-8 inches). After this point, their development will slow slightly, but they will still get substantially larger in a relatively short period, reaching around 20-25 cm (8-10) "after 16 weeks.

Maturity

Until they are about 14 months old, your cavies will continue to grow, by which time they will have reached about 20-30 cm (8-12 inches) long. They are deemed to be fully grown at this stage, and will not get any bigger. It wasn't uncommon in the past to find cavies much bigger than you find today. Thanks to so many people breeding from underage animals, they have started to get smaller in the last years.

Guinea Pig Size Chart

The following table summarizes these figures for more convenience:

Age	Size
Birth	8-10 cm (3-4 inches)
8 Weeks	15-20 cm (6-8 inches)
16 weeks	20-25 cm (8-10 inches)
14 months	20-30 cm (8-12 inches)

EYESIGHT

Their poor sense of depth gives guinea pigs a reputation for failing to see well. In fact, in comparison with human vision, guinea pigs can see 33 images per second, while humans can only see 22 images per second; this feature prevents blurred vision when a guinea pig turns its head. Guinea pigs can also see colors, which help them differentiate between red, green, and blue.

Guinea pigs are known to be able to see in the dark, and others claim they can see better in the dark than humans. But the hypothesis has not yet been proven.

Like all prey animals, guinea pigs have a wide field of sight sideways and upwards (much better than humans to detect predators easily), but they cannot see directly or straight backward.

This might not be that your guinea pig is saying what you think. Guinea pigs are animals that are wise and perceptive. Such social animals can learn to identify faces and voices, position objects, the particular treat in your pocket, and even the opening sound of the fridge door.

SENSE OF SMELL

A Guinea pig's sense of smell is important as it allows them to communicate, connect, and identify other guinea pigs and (owners) people. Owing to the many scent cells, they have their sense of smell amazing. In time, your piggy (their owners) should get used to your scent.

Guinea pigs are fastidiously clean animals that love to brush themselves and keep tidy, but when pet waste builds up inside the enclosure, it can smell — and get into his fur. Scrub the cage off once a week. With regular scooping, smells will build up in the cage, and you must thoroughly clean it up.

Smell plays a significant part in the life of a guinea pig. They use their scent to find food, and they know you. It is a well-developed feature for them as they need a strong sense of smell to pick out food. You put a very small gourmet treat in the guinea pig cage at times. Guinea pigs can't see the little treats that well, but they find the goody by sniffing it out.

You can even put a treat practically right in front of them, and the pigs have trouble seeing it many times. They sniff for it all over, until finally, they find the food.

A guinea pig learns to know you by your fragrance, so you need to be careful to use too much perfume or smell like cleaning agents do. Guinea pigs can use a mix of senses to move around in the evening. They have great vision and smell, which can be used to navigate in the night.

Chapter 2

Guinea Pig Diversity

There are only one type and color of guinea pig in nature. Over the years, however, the breeders have produced many beautiful varieties of guinea pigs from a single wild strain. How did this happen to you? How did the enormous variety that now exists develop from a single type of guinea pig?

There is a great deal of genetic diversity in every animal that reproduces sexually. This genetic diversity enables a species to adapt to changes in its environment, making it better able to survive in a changing world.

Simply put, a guinea pig inherits two genes for a specific trait, the coat color, for example — one from his father and one from his mother. Each gene is either dominant or recessive, and the coat of a guinea pig depends on which of the two genes is dominant.

When the guinea pigs became domesticated, human beings began to control the breeding of the animals. When an unusual trait arose in a guinea pig, this animal was bred with another guinea pig with a similar trait. The unusual trait often arose in the offspring of the guinea pigs, rather than being lost again, perhaps forever, as it would have been in the unusual guinea pig had married a normal guinea pig on its own.

In this way, the guinea pig breeders were able to produce the many beautiful colors and varieties described in this chapter. New and even more wonderful varieties are still being produced.

Below the fancy coat, however, a purebred guinea pig is the same as any other guinea pig and still needs a lot of affection and care.

GUINEA PIG PATTERNS AND COLORS

Guinea pigs come in different patterns and colors, each with a special beauty of their own. Within each of the following patterns, individual colors can be found.

- Agouti pattern- An agouti-colored guinea pig's hair shaft has many color lines. The agouti pattern is distinguished by two or more alternating light bands or dark ones. The eyes must be color specific to each agouti color. Wild guinea pigs all paint with the original agouti.
- Marked pattern— Guinea pigs with the marked pattern are usually white in their bodies with patterns of another color.
- Self pattern— This term is used to describe solid-colored guinea pigs that have a uniform color all over their body.
- Solid pattern— This is similar to the self-pattern, except as long as this fur does not create a pattern or mark, it may include agouti and other mixed-color furs.

Guinea pigs come in a very wide variety of colors and patterns.

While each breed has its standard breed and varieties of color, common colors can be found in many different breeds. Here are some of the most popular variations of guinea pig shades and colors.

- Beige: These kinds of guinea pigs have beige all over their bodies, including their ears and feet. Their eyes are also pink.
- Black: Black is deep in guinea pigs, a rich color that goes all the way to their skin, with matching ears and feet. The eyes are also usually black.
- Blue: Blue can be labeled as a medium shade of gray with a blue

or lavender cast. The eyes of a blue guinea pig are dark blue.

- Brindle: Brindle, a mixture also normally seen in dogs, is a combination of red and black hairs. The brindle pattern constantly shows all over the body, and the eyes are dark as well.
- Broken color: It's more of a pattern than a color. Broken guinea pigs have coats with clean-cut patches of two or more recognized colors. Exceptions include tortoiseshell, Himalayan, tortoiseshell and white, Dalmatian, and Dutch colors.
- Chocolate: The eyes are brown or dark brown with a red cast. And the deep, dark brown of a chocolate guinea pig is carried to the skin.
- Cream: This is a slight off-white that is even all over. The eyes of a cream guinea pig are always dark or red.
- Dalmatian: Like a dog of the same name, the Dalmatian guinea pigs have a coat with dark spots over a white background. The spots may be beige, black, blue, chocolate, cream, lilac, orange or red.
- Dutch: The Dutch-colored guinea pig has a dark color on the chest, neck, forelegs, and face in combination with white. The markings are different and clear.
- Golden agouti: These guinea pigs are the color of chestnut with a blue-black undercoat. The coat should have a black ticking too. The eyes are dark.
- Himalayan: Himalayan guinea pigs are white with black markings on their nose, feet, and ears. Their eyes are pink.
- Lilac: This is a medium gray color with a purplish tint spread evenly across the guinea pig's entire body, ears, and legs. The eyes are pink or dark with a ruby cast.
- Red: A Red guinea pig is a deep, rich red with matching ears and feet. The eyes are dark.
- Red-eyed orange: As the name suggests, these guinea pigs are reddish-orange with ruby red eyes.
- Roan: This color combination consists of white hairs mixed with one or two other colors. The eyes and ears match the color of the hair.

- Silver agouti: Silver agouti is a bright silver-white, which is caused by a blue-black undercoat tipped with white. These guinea pigs have dark eyes with a reddish cast.
- Tortoiseshell: Patches of red hair and patches of black hair make up an uneven checkerboard pattern over tortoiseshell guinea pigs' body. They have dark eyes.
- Tortoiseshell and white: These guinea pigs have patches of red, black, and white hair that alternate from one side of the animal to the other. Their eyes are dark.
- White: This is a pure white with no brassy or yellow tinge. The eyes are either pink or a dark color.

POPULAR BREEDS

Thirteen breeds of domesticated guinea pigs are American Cavy Breeders Association, the official registry of guinea pigs in the United States. Each breed is a wonder in and of itself, unique in color, body type, and coat of all the others. Some of them have short, round bodies. Others have figures that are longer, more streamlined.

The color of the coat, the patterns, the markings, and the texture are different in each breed. Each of these breeds is available in agouti, self, solid and distinct varieties.

Abyssinian

Abyssinian guinea pig is one of the oldest breeds of the species. His coat is covered with rosettes, a pattern that consists of radiated hair growing from the center. The rosettes are mounted one at each shoulder, four at the neck, one at each hip, and two at the rear of the guinea pig.

The Abyssinian's coat is coarse and thick and is around one and a half inches long. The Abyssinian has a medium body length to the shoulders and hindquarters, with rounded sides and plenty of widths.

Abyssinian Satin

The Abyssinian Satin Guinea pig has a shiny coat, as its name implies. He is covered with rosettes exactly like those of the Abyssinian.

American

The American is the most popular breed amongst guinea pigs and it has the appearance most people think of whenever they imagine a typical guinea pig. He has a Roman, or rounded, nose with ears that stick out from the sides of his head. His smooth coat lies close to his body.

American Satin

The American Satin is very similar to the American guinea pig, the only obvious difference is that his coat is shiny and sleek.

Coronet

The Coronet has a long coat with a large rosette or coronet which runs from the tip of his nose to the center of his ears. The ears droop slightly.

Peruvian

The Peruvian was initially known as the Angora. This breed has a thick, sweeping coat which is dragging to the ground. The Peruvian's fur, which grows down the animal's back from a center section, is thick and soft and needs a lot of grooming. Peruvian guinea pigs do their best for quick grooming if their long hair is clipped, so the animal can see where it is going.

Peruvian Satin

The Peruvian Satin is also very similar to the Peruvian, except that his coat is much silkier and more lustrous.

Silkie

Owing to his very long hair's softness, the Silkie (known as the Sheltie in Britain) is so-called. The hair grows up in a teardrop pattern from the guinea pig's nose and over his back. The Silkie takes a lot of grooming because of its luxurious coat.

Silkie Satin

The Silkie Satin is also very similar to the Silkie. The only difference between the two is the coat. The Silkie Satin's hair is very long, dense, and lustrous like the Silkie's, but it has a distinctive sheen.

Teddy

The Teddy evolved from a mutation. The breed has a thick, robust, kinky coat which is around 3/4 of an inch long. The Teddy's coat shows two different textures: plush, which is soft; and harsh, which is raw.

Teddy Satin

Just like the Teddy, the Teddy Satin's coat is short, dense, kinky, although it will reveal a glowing sheen in the right lighting.

Texel

The Texel is the newest breed that is discovered by the American Rabbit Breeders Association. The Texel's unique coat of ringlets or curls differentiates him from other cavy breeds.

White Crested

The White Crested tops his head with a single white rosette. This marking is tough to breed for, and therefore there isn't many White Crested show qualities around today. A proper crest is based around a line extending from the tip of the guinea pig's nose to the middle of its head. There are no other white hairs on the body in a show standard White Crested.

CHAPTER 3

CHOOSING YOUR GUINEA PIG

CHOOSING YOUR FIRST GUINEA PIG

When you're ready for your guinea pig, you'll want to get started on the right foot in the best way possible by looking for your new companion. A guinea pig can be purchased from a pet store or breeder, or you can adopt one. All those choices have pros and cons.

If you're working or going to school all day that likes to have a pet but still undecided on which pet you're going to choose, a guinea pig is best for you. They like to be alone in the day because most of them are quiet during the day but can still live as long as they are near another guinea pig.

Both indoors and outside, they can live as long as you keep them in cages with several rooms. They require more sensitive care, as opposed to other pet rodents.

The materials used for caring for them, too, are quite expensive. But, in comparison with other pet rodents, they can live longer years.

What makes them popular among today's rodents is that they have a unique character enjoyed by every pet owner. They are often sweet, needless regular treatment, are stylish, and often come in a range of colors. They're both sociable and friendly, so it's better if they come in pairs if you plan on taming this rodent.

When matching, it's better if you're going to match the same sexes because if you're going to have the male and female guinea pigs together, they're going to reproduce constantly. The male might hurt the pregnant guinea pig, particularly if you're unsure about their pregnancy.

Male and female guinea pigs should be separated even if their purpose is to breed them and should be exposed to mate only together in a shorter period. One of them will be younger or older than the other to live in peace.

If you have pet rabbits at home, making them your pets' companion isn't recommended. While rabbits have similar traits with guinea pigs, rabbits are so energetic that they can leap on their strong legs and reach your pets or inflict serious injury.

So, separating them is best not recommended even to the smallest race of rabbits. Interestingly, rabbits tend to have a particular mode of communicating in terms of transmitting their emotions, unlike Guinea pigs who communicate well, which is why they also have an extra guinea pig as their closest friend.

When choosing what guinea pig to tame, a cage should be considered first, since this is the place where you'll keep it for a long time to come. Next, during selection in pet stores, inspect the cage's condition since the defective keeping of these rodents inside a dirty cage can cause them serious illness without being noticed. If you've found that the cage is so disgusting, it's easier to find it in other pet shops.

The cage would allow them easy access to their food and drink. The cage should not be overcrowded with guinea pigs because it increases the risk of injury. Finally, they should look healthy as if they had a firm body, bright eyes, a clean coat, and alertness. They should be free from other unusual observations such as sticky eyes, a dirty bottom, sneezing, and sleepiness. They are also ideally at least 6-8 weeks of age before choosing them.

MALE VS. FEMALE

Both genders of guinea pigs make fantastic pets, but there are a few things to make a decision. First of all, do you have any other guinea pigs? If so, are they being neutered? Both male and female guinea pigs can be neutered, and if you don't want to be overrun by babies, you may need to neuter one or the other gender.

Neutering males or females can be done by taking a drive to the veterinarian, and it will probably cost about $50 per pet. Many experts recommend trying to keep your guinea pigs in gender-based combinations that do not require neutering, as any surgery for a guinea pig is stressful and risky.

For owners thinking of home to more guinea pigs, one crucial thing to remember when making 'what gender?' 'The decision is that it is dangerous to introduce sows to unclean males if they are a) over one-year-old, and b) have never had babies. That's because it's incredibly dangerous for these sows to get pregnant.

After all, their hip bones will have deteriorated by this age, and they'll have a hard time raising pups, if they manage it at all. Make sure you know for certain which kind of guinea pigs you have, and which gender your prospective guinea pigs are before you take the plunge.

Another factor you might want to consider is that if you have other guinea pigs, it's usually good to have more of the same sex. One of the simplest (and thus the most popular) varieties of guinea pigs is a female troupe. Like all animals, there will be some tiffs as they sort out their hierarchy, but many have found that this is the combination in which they fight the least.

All-male groups are also a common alternative, the best of which appears to be brothers—keeping guinea pigs who have known each other since birth means that they're going to be used to each other and have probably already sorted out who's in charge. If they've worked that out, so you can miss the vast majority of the negative disputes that can be very difficult to watch.

Keeping a Pair? Single?

It is best only to allow your pet to have other guinea pigs as companions. Don't ever keep your guinea pigs in the same hutch or run like rabbits because there are a risk and possibility that the guinea pigs may be bullied and seriously injured. The better combination is probably a pair or small group of the same sex, although neutered males and females may easily get along.

You may only get one guinea pig but, should you? Absolutely no. The Guinea pigs are in social nature. When their companion dies or is taken away, they tend to isolate themselves or show grief. Guinea pigs are social animals and crave the company of other pigs.

Communicating through vocalizations and touch, they coo and cuddle each other just like people greet and hug each other.A pair of pigs will play, chase, and eat together, providing round the clock companionship when they are not with you. A single pig can become very lonely, and this stress could impact their health.

WHERE TO GET IT FROM

1. Guinea Pigs can be bought from a pet shop, a Breeder or a Rescue center where you can give a full-grown piggy a home. They're very cheap to buy anywhere.

2. Wherever you buy your pigs, make sure they're fit and healthy. The babies are ready to leave their mom at about 6 weeks of age. Before you choose, watch all the pigs. Look for a healthy one that is both active and curious. All small animals are slightly nervous about people they don't know, so leave them alone when they're going to run away.

3. What to look for when you find your perfect guinea pig friend: - Smooth Glossy coat with no bald patches or scabs. -Bright eyes, clean. - The clean nose. -Silent breathing. -A plump, rounded body is resembling a brick with rounded corners! -A clean mouth with no dribbling. -The face should be gently rounded, not ratty, with a flat nose, large, bold eyes, and large, petal-shaped ears drooping.

4. If you're going to spend quality time with your guinea pig during the day, just get one or more if you want to. Guinea pigs are social, and maybe it's better to get 2 to keep each other company when you're not there.

5. Whether to choose male or female is up to you again. If you want to mate them, make sure they get on first! Female & female or male & male combinations can be great, but they can be introduced at an early age (brothers are better for boys) than they can grow together.

6. There are 13 recognized guinea pig breeds, including Abyssinian, English smooth coat, American, Coronet, Peruvian, Sheltie, Teddy, Texel, and English Crested. Peruvian, Silkie & Teddy breeds are available in Satin breeds. Satin refers to the sheen or shine of the animal coat.

To succeed in the show ring, satin animals should have brilliant coats. All breeds have the same basic characteristics of guinea pigs as the medium length with the tallest part of their shoulders. The Texel is the exception that has a short cobby body.

7. If you want to show your guinea pig, make sure you buy the right one to start doing this, as you might have to get it to stand still to be judged. Shows are held all the time but rarely advertised outside the pages of specialized publications. It would be a great place to find the perfect Guinea Pig show if that's what you're after The Abyssinian has to have eight rosettes for show quality.

8. If you have a little child, say like, under 7, it might be better to have a guinea pig as a family pet until they're old enough to take care of it themselves. It's an ideal child's pet for them to kiss and cuddle. Just when they know that this is a real thing and not a toy, you will know the right time as a parent.

9. Depending on the breed you choose; your hair may be smooth and short. Or it could have a kinked cow licked or a curly coat. Its hair could be gorgeous long flowing locks. Short-haired Guinea Pigs are easier for you to take care of if that's more of a priority for you, with only a brush now and then. With long-haired guinea pigs, you'll need to make sure they're tangle-free every day.

10. If you buy a full-size guinea pig instead of a baby, it will be around 1.3 kg-just a little more than a bag of sugar. If you feel heavy, ask that it be weighed at the shop or the breeders. A healthy pet is what you want and what your pig wants, too. They can live for about 6 or 7 years or a lot longer if they're well taken care of.

Adoption

If you're just looking for a pet guinea pig to share your life and be a companion, consider adopting one. Like dogs and cats, homeless guinea pigs are in desperate need of loving families. Every day, unwanted guinea pigs are killed in animal shelters all over the country simply because nobody wants them.

Guinea pigs in need of adoption are usually helpless creatures that once belonged to a family. They could have been bought on an impulse or were the result of an unplanned litter. No-fault of their own later discards them. They deserve a second chance with a family that will love and cares for them all their lives.

If you want to provide a home for a guinea pig who is in desperate need of one, there are some ways to do that. First, call the animal shelters in your area and ask if there are any guinea pigs for adoption. If you stop by the shelter in person and do not see any guinea pigs, be sure to ask if they are available, as many shelters keep guinea pigs in the back room away from dogs and cats. Adopting a guinea pig directly from a shelter means that you will be saving a life.

Private shelters and rescue groups are also looking for homes for guinea pigs. The Internet could be a good source for rescue groups in your area. Most rabbit rescue groups also place guinea pigs, so look for rabbit rescue organizations in your area. (If you cannot locate one of these groups on the Internet, call a local veterinarian who specializes in the treatment of exotic animals and may be able to refer you to a local group.)

If you choose to join a rescue organization, be prepared to answer a lot of questions when you call. Rescue groups seeking to place a guinea pig in a new home are responsible for asking questions about a potential foster home to determine whether the situation is right for both the guinea pig and the new owner.

When you adopt a shelter or rescue group, you may also be asked to pay a small acceptance fee. This is usually done to weed out unscrupulous people who may only be looking for a free guinea pig to feed a pet reptile or to use it for some other improper purpose. Adoption fees also help guinea pig rescuers to compensate for the cost of caring for homeless guinea pigs until new owners are found.

If you can't find a rescue group in your area and your shelter doesn't have any guinea pigs available, check out the classified ads in your local newspaper and newsletter boards in supermarkets, veterinary offices, and pet stores to find local people looking for guinea pigs.

When you search for your adoption, you will undoubtedly come across non-purebred guinea pigs in need of a home. Consider bringing one of these guinea pigs to your life. Mixed breeds are often attractive guinea pigs and have an interesting quality that most purebreds do not have: each is truly unique. If you've got your heart set on a purebred guinea pig, look for a registered in need of rescue. Many purebred guinea pigs also need a good home.

Buying a Guinea Pig

If you want to buy a guinea pig, it's important not to make an impulsive decision. All pets need and deserve the commitment of their owners. Guinea pigs can live for as long as seven years.

The adorable baby guinea pig in the window may be tiny and cute right now, but in a couple of months, she'll be a big adult who will need years of consistent, thoughtful care. Buying a pet on an impulse often results in unhappiness for the owner and a sorry fate for the animal.

If you're sure you want to own a guinea pig, the best place to buy one is a responsible breeder. Responsible breeders are guinea pig enthusiasts who research bloodlines before breeding their guinea pigs and keeping their animals clean and healthy. They are experts in their chosen breed and often show off their animals. And if you think you might want to show your pet, you must have a pedigree animal that only the breeder can provide.

Buying your pet from a responsible breeder will help ensure that you get the best guinea pig breed because each breed has its special qualities. If you buy a young, purebred guinea pig from a breeder, you'll know exactly what it will look like when it matures.

You can also see one or both of your pet's parents, giving you a chance to see what their personalities are like because their offspring are likely to have similar temperaments.

A responsible breeder will welcome you, as a prospective buyer, to their breeding operation, allowing you to see the environment in which the guinea pig has lived. This way, you'll gauge whether your prospective pet has been well cared for and is living in clean, healthy conditions.

Buying from a breeder also offers a bonus: you go home with the name and phone number of an experienced person who can answer your questions and help raise your guinea pig. If you're interested in showing your guinea pig, the breeder can help you get started in that area.

Once you have determined the breed you want, you can obtain the name and phone number of the breeder in your area by contacting one of the regional clubs in your area or by contacting the American Cavy Breeders Association. Another way to find a guinea pig breeder is to take part in a local rabbit and cavy show.

Walk around, look at the different guinea pig breeds, and talk to some of the exhibitors. Let people know that you're looking to buy a guinea pig from a breeder, and they're going to direct you to the right individuals.

PET STORES

A lot of people buy guinea pigs from pet stores. If you choose to buy your pet from a retailer, make sure that the store environment is clean, and that guinea pigs and other small animals are healthy and well-kept. Make sure you get a health guarantee for any animal you buy. Some pet stores often states the gender wrong (Mostly by mistake), which makes it difficult for a beginner to know the exact gender of that Guinea pig.

What to Expect Their Behavior

Like humans, cavies also communicate with each other through their non-verbal cues and the sounds they produce. Your pets can also show you how they feel about you through their actions and their sounds.

If you have a basic understanding of guinea pigs' behavior, you can easily develop a rewarding relationship between you and your pets. It'll be easier to train and take care of them if you know exactly how they feel every time you interact with them.

So, with that said today, we're going to look at some negative behaviors that can occur in guinea pigs. I want you to remember that every guinea pig is unique and that every guinea pig has its personality.

The behavior of your piggy is an important thing to know as a guinea pig owner. This can help tell you when he/she doesn't feel well when they're angry or happy, or even lonely.

Piggies are nature-based attention-seekers. They can get very lonely quickly, so they can make noise and hop around, sometimes just to get your attention. Your pet doesn't need to show the following types of behavior, and if they do, it's a good sign that something is wrong!

Aggression

Although the guinea pigs are generally sociable and friendly, they tend to show signs of aggression. If your cavy is angry, your teeth will start chattering and you will hear the sound of their teeth clasping together. Although there are rare instances of aggression, if they're directing it to you, you'll need to give them the space they need whenever they feel upset or upset.

Cavies rarely bite a human being. However, when they're extremely scared or upset, they might start nipping your fingers. When they show signs of aggressive behavior, you have to put them in separate cages before a fight breaks out. Before you put them in separate cages, place the towels over them to prevent them from biting you.

BITING

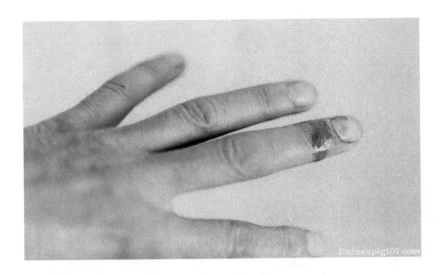

Cavies rarely bite their owners. Sometimes, they're going to start nibbling your hands like a way to communicate. As if you don't hold your cavy correctly, he'll feel scared, and he'll bite your fingers. They may also start nibbling your clothes whenever they feel the urge to go to the toilet while you're holding them. Guinea's pig behavior is so complex that you need to be sensitive in your actions to prevent miscommunication.

Your guinea pig can also bite you by accident while you're feeding it by hand. When their excitement for tasty treatment becomes too hard to control, they may accidentally nipple your finger instead of biting it. Wash your hands before feeding your cavy to prevent them from acquiring harmful bacteria.

SADNESS AND DEPRESSION

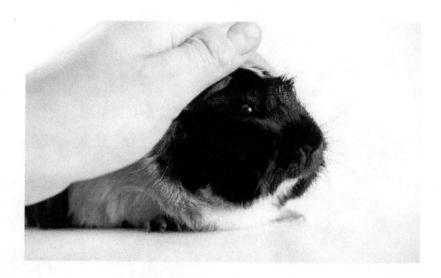

When the cavies feel depressed and frustrated, they tend to hunch in one of the corners of their cage. If your cavy seems depressed, you can make him feel better by offering him some of his favorite treats. You can also raise their spirits by giving them exciting toys that can take care of them for quite some time.

If they start refusing the food you're offering, take it to the vet. Depression is a major guinea pig behavior that needs your attention and attention. Cavies may show signs of depression every time they want to hide their illness, so you have to keep an eye on their progress.

BARBERING

Barbering is when a guinea chews on the fur of another guinea. Some people speculate that this is a sign of dominance, but I think they're just nice. Other piggies at the other end of the barbering may sit calmly as they are trimmed, others may become agitated and the other, or worse.

Begging for food

Piggies love to beg for tasty treats. As they grow up confidently, they start wheeking when they suspect that their veggies are on their way, sometimes even standing on their hind legs, just like a puppy! They're going to get excited and look in your direction with eager eyes, hoping you've seen them.

Biting of the cage bars

Some piggies are prone to biting their cage bars. Some will only do this if they want food or hear something that makes them think that food is on the way. They start wheeking, but if the chef takes too long, you'll start biting the bars out of boredom and loneliness, even if you spend a lot of time with them.

They do need a cage mate after a while, if you've owned a piggy for a while and are confident in caring for him/her, consider getting another one so that they can keep each other company. They're also going to bite the bars if their cage is small and don't get a lot of free time. The lack of exercise can make them stressed.

Please try to make a larger cage, especially if you're planning to get another piggy, and let your guinea out for a run around the house once in a while. Piggies need their freedom.

Eating Poo

If you notice your piggy duck their head underneath and see that they're chewing on something, they're eating their poo. It may sound gross to us, but it's a very natural behavior for the guineas. Rabbits will eat their poo, too. It's not the usual poo you see in the cage, it's softer and smaller. Piggies do this to re-ingest the 'soft poo' because their digestive system does not immediately extract all the vitamins from the food.

Freezing

Piggies will often stand still for a short period if they are scared or have heard a sudden, loud sound that they are unfamiliar with. It's their way of making themselves invisible and letting others in the group know. Freezing is often accompanied by a small vibrating sound, which indicates that they are scared. This behavior may happen when the phone rings or someone knocks at the door.

Licking

Like most pets, some guinea pigs love to lick you when you're holding them. Think of it as a guinea pig kisses. Not all piggies do that, about 3 out of 6 piggies love kissing. Some people think it's because our skin is salty and they enjoy the taste, I'm not all that convincing, and I think it's more of affectionate behavior.

The Mating Dance

Both males and females participate in this dance. They will swing their hips back and forth and make a vibrating sound known as a motorboat. Don't be alarmed if your female piggy starts a mating dance with another female; she's probably just feeling hormonal.

Mounting

Usually, this is seen as sexual behavior, but it can also be a sign of dominance towards another guinea. A dominant male can do this to a submissive male, usually, when they first meet, they're just sorting out who the boss is, or the king of the cage. A female may also mount another female if she is in season or if a neutered male does not pay attention. It's all very normal, so don't worry if you see the same sex piggies mounting each other.

However, if males do it to each other, watch out for signs of aggression, you don't want a fight to break out. The actual act of mounting only takes a few quick seconds, but the mounting starts again after a rest. Before the mounting starts, there might be a bit of a chase involved.

The piggy that is being chased may sometimes complain and become annoyed. As long as you don't see any aggressive behavior, it sounds much worse than it is. Being constantly chased can be exhausting and stressful, so if you have a spare cage, it might be a good idea to separate your guinea pigs so that they can have some peace for a while.

CHAPTER 4

BRINGING YOUR GUINEA PIG HOME

You've chosen a guinea pig that you're going to adopt or buy. However, before you bring him home, you need to prepare for his environment. Shopping and setting up all the equipment and supply you need for your guinea pig before arriving will make his introduction to your home less stressful for both of you.

Once you have chosen Guinea to be a pet in your home, it is important to make sure that its surroundings are safe. Just as any pet needs time to play, fresh food, water, and toys, so does your Guinea Pig. Bringing your guinea pigs home to a safe environment is very important to both you and your new pet.

Common sense plays a huge role in preparing and maintaining your pet's safe and happy home. It is also important to be educated about the type of pet you bring to your home, as this will help you maintain your health and happiness daily. Not a lot of time is needed, but it should be taken into account to ensure your pet's positive welfare.

First and foremost, the choice of a healthy Guinea Pig is the first step. Knowing and understanding some of the basic needs is different. Guinea Pigs love to play, so they need space. When choosing your cage, you might want to get the next size so that there's room for both your pet and their toys and places to hide for rest.

Besides, if you're not going to give a lot of one at a time, you might want to consider getting two so that there's going to be a company at all times (but that's not necessary).

Bringing your guinea pigs home to a safe environment is very important not only to you but especially to your pet. A safe cage or a safe area for your home, clean food (mainly fresh hay) and water should be provided every day, a good place for your pet to hide, such as a box upside down or a tube that has smooth edges and toys to play with that don't have parts that can easily come off or too small to cause choking.

Safety comes into play, too, if you already have animals in your house. Dogs may not necessarily be of concern, but if you own a cat, you may want to review the area and the housing you provide to ensure that both the cat and the Guinea pig are not harmed.

It is not difficult to ensure that your home is a haven for your new pet, just look at the area that will be designated for your new pet and see if there are any possible negatives within that area. If there is one, obviously move the cage or housing to another, more secure area within your home.

The best thing you can do since Guinea pigs are unable to speak is to try and be one step ahead of their needs and wants. As with any pet you may bring to your home, it is extremely important to be a responsible caregiver. Bringing your guinea pigs home to a safe environment should be a priority in the preparation list for the new pet.

Indoor Housing

Even though your indoor guinea pig is going to have the same roof over his head as you are, he still needs his private retreat. A cage will provide security for your guinea pig (and your home!), as well as privacy and a haven.

The indoor guinea pig cages are available in pet stores and through catalogs, and there are a wide variety of styles available. Look for one made of sturdy wire with a removable bottom tray. Your guinea pig is not going to be able to gnaw on the wire, and the removable tray will make cleaning easier. The wire will also give your pet the ventilation and light it needs.

A solid, rust-proof metal or hard plastic floor is suitable for a guinea pig. While the wire mesh bottom can make cleaning the cage easier, it's not very safe for your guinea pig because the legs can easily get caught in it.

Also, the wire floors can lead to sore legs and hocks. If you insist on a cage with a wire floor, a solid area made of wood (any kind except redwood, which is toxic) must be provided somewhere in the cage so that the guinea pig can find relief from the wire bottom.

The indoor cage should be large enough for the guinea pig to stretch out and move in while also accommodating the nest box, food and water accessories, and a toy or two. The cage's height should allow the guinea pig to stand up on his hind legs without touching the top of his head.

Look for a cage that is robustly constructed and easy to disassemble for cleaning. It should also have a door on top so that you can reach inside and a door on the side so that the guinea pig can get in and out of the cage if he wants to.

Nest Box

Guinea pigs are, by nature, burrowing animals. They live under the ground in the wild, in dens, they dig themselves. These burrows give them a sense of security. For this reason, guinea pigs who live above the ground like pets enjoy having nest boxes, a substitute for burrows, inside their cage.

The nest box is a small enclosure that contains the animal's bedding and has a hole cut into it. It's a safe place to sleep and hide. A cardboard box would work well as a nest box, but most guinea pigs would quickly chew it to pieces so that wood would be preferred. (They're going to chew that, too, but not as fast.)

Commercial nest boxes are available through pet supply outlets and mail-order catalogs specializing in small animal supplies. Or maybe you can build your own. Just make sure that the wood has never been treated with anything toxic.

Your guinea pigs nest box should be large enough for the animal to turn around while several inches of bedding is in place. Ensure that the entrance to the nest box is large enough for your guinea pig to get in easily and that one side of the box is removable so that you can clean it. There should be no sharp edges in the box.

Location

When you decide where to put your guinea pigs cage in your house, remember that extreme temperatures are dangerous. Don't put your guinea pigs cage in a spot where the sun shines directly on it. Avoid keeping it close to a radiator, stove, fireplace, or another heating element.

Cold drafts can be deadly, too. Keep your guinea pigs cage away from doors and windows where winter drafts can leak. Try to keep your guinea pigs cage off the floor during cold weather, too, as cold air tends to lie near the ground, creating drafts.

Avoid putting your guinea pigs cage in dark or damp areas. Basements and garages are not suitable for guinea pigs, as they usually have minimal light, poor ventilation, and excessive moisture. Garages are also dangerous, as guinea pigs are sensitive to car-exhaust fumes.

Try to find a place in your home where your guinea pig can watch household activity without being unduly disturbed. You want your guinea pig to feel like he's part of a family, so his cage needs to be in a room where people come and go. But don't put him in such a busy place that he's never going to be able to rest or relax. Be especially careful not to place the cage near the TV, stereo, or radio. Hearing a guinea pig is very sensitive, and a lot of noise can be very disturbing.

Indoor vs. Outdoor Housing

Before you get a guinea pig, you should decide whether your pet will be living with you in your home or outdoors in the yard. It's best indoors, for all the reasons I'm going to explain. However, guinea pigs can live indoors or outdoors, and the items you need to have on hand before your pet arrives will vary slightly depending on where your guinea pig lives.

It's impossible to appreciate life with a guinea pig unless you keep it in your home. Like dogs and cats, guinea pigs are companion animals with unique and interesting personalities. If you're not living with a guinea pig, day in and day out, you're never going to get to know him.

The guinea pig isn't going to know you that well, either. If your guinea pig is out most of the time, the two of you will lead separate lives. You're going to miss getting him to sleep on your lap while watching TV and watching you from the floor while you're eating your dinner. People who live with indoor guinea pigs enjoy these antics and more of their pets.

There are many other practical reasons to keep a guinea pig indoors. Guinea pigs who remain inside tend to live longer than the outdoor guinea pigs. Bad weather and predators are responsible for the deaths of many outdoor guinea pigs. These are the consequences of living outdoors that even conscientious owners cannot always control.

Illness is a major cause of death among outdoor guinea pigs, mainly because outdoor pets are more difficult to monitor. At first, signs of an illness can be subtle, and since outdoor guinea pigs spend less time with their owners, it may be a day or so before the owner recognizes the illness. In the case of fast-moving diseases, a delay of even one day can cost a guinea pig. It's a wise decision to keep your guinea pig indoors. Even guinea pigs who have been living outside for years can acclimate to indoor life.

Why Indoor Housing Is Best for Them

Guinea pigs are better kept indoors for several reasons. Cavies prefer similar temperatures to humans, so the constant temperature they will have at home will help keep them healthy and happy.

Because you'll see them more often, if they get sick, you'll notice a lot faster than if they were outside. This means that you can get the medical attention they need faster, which can save them from a bad illness.

For indoor guinea pigs, it is recommended that either the guinea pig habitat cage or the C&C cage be the ideal housing for them, and either of these is much easier to clean than a hutch.

It's very important that your guinea pig cage is large enough. Some cages advertised for guinea pigs don't give them the space they need. They like to run around, or they're going to get depressed.

Guinea pigs love the company, so you need to consider having a pair of piggies seriously. You can house more than two together, but you'll need a modular C&C cage for three or more guinea pigs, as most ready-made cages don't have enough room for more than two cavies.

The recommended cage size for 2 guinea pigs is 120 cm x 60 cm x 45 cm (or 4 ft x 2 ft x 1.5 ft). Checking the spacing between the wires of the cage is not too large. If they are, they could either escape, or they could hurt themselves by getting stuck.

Ideal Temperature

About 65-75 degrees Fahrenheit is the ideal temperature range for guinea pigs. Guinea pig housing can be situated a little far from strong heat sources such as direct sunlight, fireplaces, wood stoves, and heating vents.

Room temperatures below 70 or over 90 degrees Fahrenheit (Guinea pigs will quickly grow respiratory illnesses if the temperature falls below 65 degrees Fahrenheit.) bedding made of cedar or air-dried pine shavings that are harmful to small animals (if wood shavings are used, aspen or kiln-dried pine will be used).

Guinea Pig Proofing Your Home

Because guinea pigs are gnawing animals and have an innate need to chew, it is vitally important to prove your home to guinea pigs before you let your pet run loose. In addition to providing your guinea pig with toys that he can chew on, you will also need to devise ways to keep him from gnawing on household items for home and animal health.

Electrical cords pose the greatest threat to the safety of your guinea pig and should be a primary concern. Guinea pigs will chew through cords, electrocuting themselves, and creating a fire hazard in your home.

You can protect your home and your guinea pig by moving the cords out of reach. Cords that cannot be moved should be covered with plastic aquarium-type tubes. Slit the tubing lengthwise and lay the cord inside to do this. Or try wrapping the spiral cable cord, which is available in electronics stores.

Guinea pigs chew on anything made of wood, so wood moldings, furniture legs, and other chewable that is attractive to your guinea pig can be covered with thick plastic or treated with a dissuasive scent. Perfume and cologne are repugnant to guinea pigs who have a strong sense of smell.

You can also use store-bought repellents made to keep other pets away. Not all guinea pigs will be repulsed by this, however, and you may have to resort to covering areas with un-chewable surfaces.

Another important aspect of guinea pig testing in your home is to take a look at all the places where your guinea pig could be caught or hidden. Since guinea pigs are curious animals, your pet will want to explore every corner of your house.

Look around for guinea pig-sized spaces that your pet can escape through or get trapped in. Block these areas securely. And while you're looking at the house, make sure that toxic household chemicals and trash bags are well hidden from your pet.

You can prevent much of the destruction that guinea pigs can cause and keep your new pet safe by looking at your home from a guinea pig's point of view. Get all fours down and look around. Do you see loose electrical wires, cords hanging from the blinds, chewy shoes on the floor? Your guinea pig is going to see them too!

In all the rooms your guinea pig will be allowed in:

- Get plastic trashcans with tight-fitting lids.
- Spray wooden moldings and furniture legs with a scent deterrent, or cover them with a non-chewable surface.
- Keep all household cleaners, medicines, vitamins, shampoos, bath products, perfumes, makeup, nail polish remover, and other personal products in cupboards that close securely.
- Cover or tack up electrical cords; consider childproof covers for unused outlets.
- Knot or tie up any dangling cords from curtains, blinds, and the telephone.
- Put all houseplants out of reach.
- Pick up all chewable items, including television and electronics remote controls, cellphones, shoes, socks, slippers and sandals, food, dishes, cups and utensils, toys, books, and magazines, etc.

that can be chewed on.
- Block off all nooks, cracks, and crevices where a guinea pig could hide.

CAGE AMENITIES

Whether your guinea pig lives indoors or outdoors, it will need more than just a cage to live a comfortable and healthy life. There are some cage accessories that you should buy before he arrives.

The food bowl of your guinea pig is very important and should be chosen wisely. Don't use any of the old dishes you have in the cupboard, as the guinea pigs chew or knock on the wrong kind of food container. Instead, take a trip to your local pet food store and buy a ceramic crock made specifically for pets. Ceramic crocks are chew-resistant and difficult to knock over.

Keep in mind the size of your guinea pig when you buy a food crock. Don't buy a dish that's too small for a guinea pig to put his head in or too big to get in comfortably.

Another option is a metal bowl that is attached to the side of the cage.

When selecting a metal bowl, be sure it's not so deep that the guinea pig can't reach it all the way. Ensure that the bowl is attached to the side of the cage at a low enough level to allow easy access.

A bottle of water is another necessity for your guinea pigs cage. Gravity water bottles are easy to find in pet stores. These are the best kind of water containers for guinea pigs, because they can't be knocked over, and the water stays clean in the bottle. Make sure the bottle of water you're buying isn't too small (it should be more than 8 ounces).

You want your guinea pig to drink as much water as possible to keep it healthy, and a small bottle will need to be filled more than once a day. Also, make sure there's a metal ball in the tip of the water bottle. This will keep you from leaking into your guinea pigs cage.

Another important item for the cage is the hay rack. Hay is a vital part of your guinea pig's daily diet. The hay rack will hold the hay in place so that it won't be scattered throughout the cage. Hay racks are usually made of metal and are attached to the top of the cage. The guinea pig can pull the strands of hay out of the rack whenever he gets the urge to munch.

There should be a supply of food on hand. Find out what your guinea pig ate in his previous home and start offering him the same things. If you need to change your diet, you'll have to do so for a few weeks to avoid upsetting your digestion.

You're going to need a litter box and a litter if you're planning to try a litter box to train your guinea pig. A small litter box made for a cat may be good for a guinea pig, provided it is not too large.

You're going to want bedding available for your guinea pig, too. Guinea pigs enjoy sleeping on wood shavings, scraped paper, processed ground corn cob, and commercial bedding pellets.

Wood shavings, shredded paper, corn cob, and bedding pellets made, especially for small animals, can be purchased in any pet food store. (Some experts believe that cedar shavings can be detrimental to the respiratory system of a guinea pig. Many guinea pig owners prefer to use other, less aromatic, bedding for their pets.)

Since guinea pigs are gnawing mammals, you will need to have safe chewing blocks in your guinea pig cage. Untreated wood can be used, but the safest items for your guinea pig to gnaw are commercially prepared wood blocks or chews available in pet stores. These gnawing toys are available in various colors and shapes, made especially for chewing animals, and are safe and cheap.

A lot of people are surprised to learn that Guinea pigs love to play with toys. A toy for a guinea pig can be anything from an empty toilet roll of paper to a small cardboard box. Having a few items on hand when your guinea pig arrives will help him to feel at home in his new environment. While he may not be playing with these items right away, he will appreciate their presence as soon as he becomes acclimated to his new environment.

ACCLIMATING THE NEWCOMER

This will be an exciting moment when your New Guinea pig comes home for the first time. Everyone in the family will be eager to feel his soft fur and watch him explore his new environment. As exhilarating as this moment is, it is important to realize that your guinea pig will have a different perspective.

Put yourself in his place for a moment: he's just been taken out of his familiar surroundings, trapped in a box, and sent away to a place he's never seen before. It's all new to him, and it's a huge size! There's little doubt he's going to be overwhelmed. Because of the guinea pig's instinct to always be alert to predators, you may notice that your new pet seems shy and frightening.

Remember, this is the normal behavior of guinea pigs. Your pet will need a lot of love, patience, and understanding to learn how to relax. Be sure to give him a place to hide when he's introduced to his new situation. This is going to provide him with much-needed security.

The nicest way to let your guinea pig get used to his new home is to leave him alone for a while. Place him in his cage that you've been equipped with food, water, and everything he's going to need to survive, and then let him check things out in privacy for a couple of hours.

After your guinea pig has had a chance to get used to his new cage, you can begin to observe him softly. Speak to him softly to reassure him that everything is all right and to let him get used to your voice.

If you have children, it's a good time to teach them how to treat their new guinea pig. Explain to them that their new pet needs peace to learn to feel comfortable in his new home. If your children are eager to show their New Guinea pigs to their friends, ask their friends to visit one or two of them at a time so they can't scare the animal. They should be as quiet as possible when they're close to the new pet.

Guinea's pigs' ears are very sensitive, and loud noises can be frightening. Be sure your kids understand that they're not supposed to handle a guinea pig right away. Because the New Guinea pig is going to be fearful and skittish, any attempt to hold him back may injure the guinea pig. It's vital that you first learn the right way to handle a guinea pig, and then teach your child to do that.

Once your child has learned how to handle techniques, always check to make sure it's done correctly. The skeleton of a guinea pig is fragile, and dropping a squirming guinea pig to the ground could result in fatal injury.

It's also important to keep other pets away from the New Guinea pig while it's getting used to its surroundings. Your guinea pig needs time to adjust to his new life, and it's best to introduce him one step at a time to each element. At first, keep his cage in an area that is somewhat isolated, where cats and dogs can't bother him. Later, when he feels more comfortable, you can have him meet your other pets.

How to Build a Bond

A tame guinea pig is a much happier and more enjoyable companion for a variety of reasons. Taking the time to tie your piggy properly would guarantee a much healthier relationship over your pet's lifetime. They're not only going to be a better pet, but they're also going to have a better quality of life, and they're coming to enjoy your company and seek your attention.

A super tame guinea pig can be almost dog-like in temperament, always following his owner around like a puppy. A guinea pig who loves being with you and getting love is a great pet. Also, a tame guinea pig is much more workable and will learn new tricks faster than one that is nervous about you and your environment.

Also, to better interact with your guinea pig, you should be prepared to spend time with them regularly, regardless of the method(s) you want to use.

Spend Lots of Time with Your Piggy!

The easiest way to train and communicate with a guinea pig is to spend a lot of time with them in a constructive way. Essentially, this means that you let them come to you and give vegetables whenever they approach. The enclosed setting, such as a training pen or a dry bathtub with towels spread out, is a perfect place to sit with and let them come to you. Give some food when they meet you, so they equate you with something good rather than a possible threat.

When your piggy doesn't come close enough to take the food out of your pocket, gently throw the food at them if they come in your direction, and wait until they come a little closer each time. Speak to them in a positive voice and give their favorite veggie treats. Hanging out with your piggy often and regularly is the secret to getting a sweet and friendly piggy and establishing a close bond.

Once your piggy is confident approaching you and taking food from your side, you will start making them come to your lap to get food, first by rewarding them for putting their front paws up, then luring them to your lap with food. If you can get your piggy to do this consistently because of their veggies, you'll be in a very good position to start teaching tricks, as this shows that the guinea pig is comfortable around you and will follow a lure in the form of food.

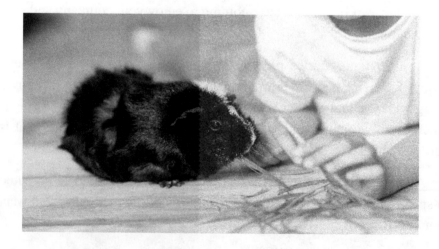

If your guinea pig doesn't eat any vegetables in your presence, you can still form a beneficial relationship with yourself by draping a blanket over your leg and on the floor to form a tent for a guinea pig hide in. It gives the guinea pig a place to hide and feel relaxed while still getting used to being close to you, rather than running away and hiding from you.

Many people placed the guinea pig on their lap with a blanket or a baggy sweater and let them cover themselves inside. This is another way to keep the guinea pig happy in your presence before they're afraid of you.

Guinea Pigs That Run When You Try to Pick Them Up

As prey animals, guinea pigs are instinctively nervous of shadows, and anything coming at them from above. In addition to this, guinea pigs do have poor eyesight and appear to spook quickly as a protective reflex. It is also a good idea to talk to your piggy whenever you are approaching their cage and reaching in, so they know it is you. It's always a good idea to pet the guinea pig a little before lifting them and giving them a heads-up of your intentions.

Regardless of how comfortable and familiar your guinea pig is with being picked up, or how often you let your piggy know of your intentions, he/she most definitely still be a little wary of being picked up. It is natural for a prey animal, and such is to be expected from them. They will be more comfortable with their feet on the ground, in control of their actions.

To keep piggies comfortable with being transported from their cage to the floor and from the floor back to their cage, you can just teach them how to hop into their pigloo (turned upside down). This is one of the best (and easiest) ways to move them from place to place.

It can be beneficial for both you and the guinea pigs too; the piggies are happier if they are being moved around this way, and you don't need to chase them around to get them in or out of their cage. To teach them this, you can just start by training them outside of their cage, luring them into the pigloo with a treat and rewarding them, until they go in on their own as soon as they see the upside-down pigloo.

Socializing with New People & Different Environments

Anyone who has had a guinea pig knows who your piggy can be the sweetest little rascal while hanging out with you, running up to you and checking out love and sweets, and then totally vanish the second a stranger enters the house. Or the piggy happily explores every corner of the space they are used to and freezes in terror when taken to a new room five steps away from their normal location.

Piggies are conditioned into their routine, and everything in it and is thrown off when everything changes, just in the least.

You may want to get the guinea pig used to other people and locations for some reason. If you teach your guinea pig tricks and want to show us what your piggy can do, you're bound to want him/her to be socialized a little with other people. Otherwise, the guinea pig is unable to do any tricks with anyone watching.

To socialize the piggy with other people, you should simply have another person sit in an enclosed space with your piggy and have the person handle the guinea pig whenever the piggy comes near them. You can do this a couple of times for each person, and you can replicate the cycle for a few different people.

Getting a guinea pig used to new places is more tedious and time-consuming; however, the more places you get your piggy acquainted with, the more versatile they ought to be with new places later on. To acquaint a guinea pig with another room or territory, give beginning a shot by putting a pen up to fence off a little segment, to let the piggy wander in only a little zone of the new room.

Bring the guinea pig back a couple of various occasions, causing the space they need to investigate somewhat greater each time. A progressively sure guinea pig may be glad to investigate the entire region simultaneously, so if you have a piggy like that, you can give them access to more space immediately on the off chance that you need. It will most likely take any guinea pig a long time to be agreeable in another spot; however, so heaps of time and persistence is basic.

HANDLING YOUR GUINEA PIG

Guinea pigs do not like to be lifted and held unless they are gradually taught to tolerate it. If your guinea pig has not been kept so much in his life, it will take expertise and patience to embrace it. Because guinea pigs are not natural climbers, your pet would feel uncomfortable and nervous when raised off the ground. As a result, he can struggle frantically.

A fall can seriously injure a guinea pig. For this purpose, you must learn to carry your guinea pig properly and safely.

Before you begin practicing picking up and carrying your guinea pig, be sure to wear protective clothing. Bare skin and unclipped guinea pig nails don't mix!

The best way to pick up a guinea pig is to place one hand under the animal so that the legs are on either side of your hand, and then lift it with the other hand to hold the back. Holding a guinea pig against your chest in this way helps you feel secure. If you start fighting during the handling process, bend down to your knees.

This is going to keep him from falling too far if you lose your grip on him. If you have children, keep a close eye on them when they want to handle a guinea pig. Teach them the right way to lift and carry a guinea pig, and always supervise them when they do it.

Because guinea pigs are fragile and improper handling can result in a severely injured animal, very young children should not be allowed to pick up or carry guinea pigs. Petting a guinea pig while he's on the floor, all four feet safely, is a better approach when very young children are involved.

Remember always to treat your guinea pig gently and carefully when handling it. Since it is not natural for a guinea pig to be lifted and carried, you will need patience and kindness to help your new pet accept this type of handling.

SPECIAL GUIDE FOR KIDS AND PARENTS

Guinea pigs and children do make great friends. But you need to ask yourself if your kids are old enough to learn how to handle the guinea pig properly and treat him with respect. These are small animals, and they can easily be hurt. Very young children cannot understand that a guinea pig needs to be held a certain way and that a guinea pig should not be picked up without adult supervision.

Responsible older children will even be able to take a large role in caring for a guinea pig. But you will still have to take responsibility for the pet, no matter what your children promised when you got him. Even though they have the best intentions, most children do not have the attention span required for the care of a guinea pig, who may live as long as seven years.

Although a parent should never expect a child to take full

responsibility for any pet, allotting guinea pig chores is one way to let everyone in the family participate in the pet's life. Set realistic expectations for your kids based on their maturity.

A younger child may help out by offering the guinea pig a treat (such as fruit or green vegetables) every day, while an older child can be expected to feed the guinea pig and check his water supply daily. Whatever your child's responsibility, praise him or her for a job well done. You don't want to make the guinea pig a topic your child would rather stop. So note that you will still be present to track the pet's well-being.

No child should be given unsupervised responsibility for any animal. Children cannot be expected to identify symptoms of disease in a guinea pig or to be able to assess the guinea pig's well-being. An adult will still be the pet's primary caregiver, ready to take on the child's duties should they neglect them.

Otherwise, it is the poor guinea pig who struggles in your attempt to teach your child responsibility.

To help care for the guinea pig, children can have fun with these pets. Your child could even make toys for guinea pigs out of toilet paper tubes, paper bags, empty tissue boxes, and other safe objects. Let your child use their imagination. One other fun guinea pig activity is simple observation.

This is a great way to get your child to learn about animal behavior in general and rodent behavior in specific. Another nice way to get your child involved with their pet is to join a 4-H program. Younger children will also have a great deal of fun with a guinea pig, but they need to be watched. A guinea pig is a great way to teach them to respect other living things.

Tell them how to be gentle with their beloved guinea pig. Let them pet the guinea pig on the floor, but don't allow them to pick him up. Young children may get shocked or irritated, or may just not be able to handle the guinea pig properly. As a result, the guinea pig could get dropped and injured. Instead, keep the guinea pig yourself and encourage your child to pet him.

INTRODUCING OTHER PETS

Guinea pigs are indeed very social animals that can get along with other pets, especially cats, dogs, rabbits, and other guinea pigs. Nevertheless, whether there is peace in a particular multi-pet household depends primarily on the individual animals involved and the owner.

If your guinea pig is going to live happily in your home, he will have to get used to your other pets. It can take quite some time, patience, and commitment to teaching your dog or cat to get along with a guinea pig. Never push pets on one another, and always supervise your animals when they are together. Ensure you pay particular attention to this aspect of guinea pig ownership because your guinea pig's life depends on it.

GUINEA PIGS AND DOGS

Once it comes to dogs, guinea pig owners have to take proper care. Dogs are predators, and guinea pigs are prey animals. It's instinctual for dogs to chase and kill guinea pigs, and it's instinctive for guinea pigs to fear dogs and run from them. If you are going to keep both a guinea pig and a dog, you need to be aware of this intrinsic tension.

The safest way to manage a dog-guinea pig relationship is never to allow the dog and the guinea pig to be loose together in your home or backyard. Neither dog can be fully trusted with a small animal like a guinea pig. A dog will kill a guinea pig in a few seconds.

Some dogs can be taught to value a caged guinea pig, however. You should be instructed not to annoy the guinea pig while he is in his cage and leave you alone while you are holding the guinea pig in the arms. If you already have a dog and want to bring a guinea pig into your home, you should consider a few points.

First of all, think about your dog's personality. Is she a mellow, old couch potato who is hard-pressed to get upset or excited? Or is she a younger, more active dog? Dogs that are older and calmer generally do better when new pets are added. Be patient, though. The mellowest of dogs will unexpectedly come to life when she sees a guinea pig scurrying around the room.

If you have a small, easily excitable dog, guinea pig ownership can still work out for you, if you can handle your dog. During the introduction process, you will have to be able to control your dog's excitement. If she ignores you when you call her and marches to the beat of her drummer, you will have a problem.

If your dog is controllable, think of her past interactions with other species. Was she violent against cats? Does she like to chase squirrels and other small animals? Have you helped her do this? If your answer to these questions is yes, you will have a difficult time teaching your dog that the New Guinea pig is off-limits, since she has already learned that it's okay to chase smaller animals.

You can certainly give it a try, but you may have to consider keeping the two animals apart forever or simply passing on guinea pig ownership.

Consider the dog's breed as well. Many terriers, some types of hounds, and some other breeds have been bred for hundreds of years to hunt small mammals. If your dog is one of these hunting breeds, keep in mind that one looks at your New Guinea pig could trigger previously dormant hunting instincts in your dog. Under this case, you will have to try even harder to train your dog to suppress her innate urges and not torment your guinea pig.

When you have determined your dog is managed enough to try making friends with a guinea pig, you should begin the slow process of adding the two animals.

Make sure your new guinea pig has had enough time to get used to his new home before introducing him to your family. Once he seems comfortable, start the proceedings by putting your dog on a leash and asking an adult whom the dog respects to control her.

Enable your dog to enter the guinea pigs cage quietly slowly. If the dog gets rambunctious, correct her by saying, "No!" and quickly pulling back on the rope. If the dog stands still, compliment her and let her know that this is the kind of action you expect from her when she is close to the guinea pig. If your guinea pig first lays eyes on your dog, he will most certainly be scared.

He would probably dive into his nest box and run. Let him remain there because he will feel much more comfortable. Finally, if the dog behaves in a nonthreatening way, the guinea pig may become braver and more curious, eventually venturing out of the nest box to explore.

When the dog and the guinea pig are relaxed with each other in this situation, and the guinea pig is used to getting out of his cage without the dog present, you can try holding the guinea pig in your arms the dog present. Start your session indoors by putting the dog on a leash. You may also want to muzzle her, just to be safe.

Take your guinea pig out of the cage and hold him in your arms as you move slowly across the room. Reassure the guinea pig with a calming voice while the person keeping the leash encourages the dog to watch you. If the dog acts aggressively, correct her by saying, "No" and pulling back on the leash. When the dog sits there and silently listen, thank her.

The guinea pig may become scared by the dog's presence and the fact that he is outside of his cage and may struggle to get away. The dog's first reaction would be to get excited about this.

Teach the dog that this is not appropriate, and don't encourage her to run up and climb on you. Using the dog's obedience training, instruct her to sit, and she can come to realize that this is a special animal that cannot be hurt in any way. Repeat these exercises before the dog gets the message. (Muzzling your dog when the guinea pig is in your arms is highly recommended before you are fully sure that she does not hurt the guinea pig.)

This can take a couple of months, but if you are diligent, you will see results. Regardless of how well your dog behaves with your guinea pig, never leave the two alone loose in your house or yard. This is for your guinea pig's health.

GUINEA PIGS AND CATS

Cats are typically better companions for guinea pigs than dogs, mostly because the two animals are a little smaller in size. Though cats are predators and may be inclined to chase guinea pigs, they are less capable of doing damage than a dog, which can kill a guinea pig with one snap of her jaws. It is unlikely that a cat would be so aggressive against a guinea pig that the two cannot be housemates.

When preparing to introduce your cat and your guinea pig, start by buying a harness for your cat and getting her used to wearing it. Keeping your cat in a harness during the introduction outside your guinea pigs cage will allow you power over her should she become violent. You should always have a water gun nearby if your cat gets out of control, and you need to squirt her to deter inappropriate actions.

Start by showing the guinea pig to your cat while the guinea pig is still in his cage. The two animals will be very wary of each other at first, and the guinea pig may hide in his nest box. When your cat behaves tentatively and does not act aggressively against the guinea pig, reward her with praise and treatment.

When she hisses at the guinea pig and runs away, ignore it. She will probably come back to investigate and will finally get used to the intruder. If the cat reaches her arm into the cage and tries to get at the guinea pig, squirt her rump with the water pistol from a distance. It will let her know that this kind of action against the guinea pig reaps negative consequences.

Once the two animals begin to ignore each other, you'll know you are ready for the next step. Let your guinea pig out of his cage indoors, with your cat in the harness being carried by another adult. When the guinea pig runs, the cat can act as though she wants to chase the guinea pig. Don't make it. Instead, keep the cat still and let her watch the guinea pig moves around the room until she gets used to the idea that she's not allowed to chase.

You will need to continue these get-acquainted sessions frequently before both animals are relaxed with each other. It may take some time, but in most cases, your efforts will pay off. Of course, the safest way to have a cat and a guinea pig in the same home are to keep the guinea pig caged or secure in your arms while the cat is present. Never, under any circumstances, leave your cat and guinea pig alone together unsupervised.

OTHER GUINEA PIGS

Fostering cohabitation between two guinea pigs can be difficult. In the wild, guinea pigs live with their species in complex societies. Whenever a guinea pig is introduced to a member of his species, the two animals have to find out exactly where either one falls in the pecking order.

The first step toward a good relationship among guinea pigs is spaying and neutering, especially in the case of two males. Raging hormones can cause an intact male guinea pig to fight with another guinea pig he might otherwise get along with. Spaying and neutering both female and male guinea pigs removes hormones from the equation, rendering them calmer and more docile.

When trying to decide whether two guinea pigs will become friends, keep in mind that gender can be an important aspect. Spayed females and neutered males tend to get along better than other gender combinations, although two intact females have been known to become good friends.

Adding two guinea pigs is different from adding a dog and a guinea pig or a cat and a guinea pig. Guinea pigs see other guinea pigs differently than they do members of other species and are capable of behaving much more aggressively with each other. In many situations, guinea pigs who are strangers will seriously fight. This is why it is necessary to allow them to get used to each other gradually.

Begin by finding a neutral territory where neither guinea pig has had a chance to stake a claim. This can be a room in the house where neither has been or even the back seat of a parked car.

Placing the guinea pigs on unclaimed turf will temper their instinctive urge to defend their territory. Keep the guinea pigs in their cages first, and put the cages next to each other on neutral turf. Leave them together like this as often as possible.

Once their tensions have subsided and they seem less hostile toward each other through the bars of their cages, they take them out and get close to each other, still in the neutral place. There might be some fighting, but you can break it up by squirting a water pistol at the two culprits. Provided you have not mixed two intact males, the guinea pigs will eventually work things out and will learn to tolerate each other or, hopefully, become fast friends. Again, this is much more likely if the guinea pigs are spayed or neutered.

Keep in mind that putting intact male and female guinea pigs together will soon result in multiple litters of baby guinea pigs. Since there are still more guinea pigs than there are homes for them, the most responsible thing to do is stop separating males and females together. The problem of reproduction can be overcome, of course, by getting the animals spayed or neutered.

LITTER BOX TRAINING

The guinea pig's denning impulse makes him a candidate for litter box training; guinea pigs, very much like cats and rabbits, prefer not to foul the area where they eat and sleep. Some guinea pigs can be trained to use a litter box, although they are not as good as rabbits. If you would like to try litter box training your guinea pig, have patience, and accept that your pet may never be 100 percent reliable.

The essential things to bear in mind when litter box training a guinea pig are consistency and praise. Never scold your guinea pig for not using the litter box since this will only scare and confuse him. Another crucial idea is to work slowly, starting your guinea pig in a small space and, ideally, extending to more and more rooms of the whole building.

Most guinea pig owners use organic cat litter for their guinea pig's litter box, especially brands made from corn, paper, wheat, or grass. Keep away from clay and wood-based litters, as these appear to be dusty and can cause respiratory problems for guinea pigs. Some pet supply stores specializing in small mammals will carry litter made just for them. This is the best type to buy. You may also use a straw on top of a newspaper layer as litter, but it will be less absorbent than most commercially produced brands.

Start Small

Start the litter box training process in a very small area, preferably the guinea pigs cage. Put a small litter box (a plastic washing-up bin with low sides that's big enough for him to stand in comfortably) in the corner of your pet's cage, attached to the side with a clip or twistable wire so you can remove it for cleaning.

Try to place the box in the area of the cage that your guinea pig tends to use as a bathroom and far away from his food, water, and nest box. Put some fecal pellets in the box to help give him the right idea and then add a handful of hay to a corner of the box to encourage your guinea pig to use it.

Seek to keep an eye on your guinea pig while he is in his cage. When you see him defecate in the litter box, offer him a treat as a reward. Don't be surprised if the guinea pig sits in the box and munches on the hay you've put in it, as guinea pigs will also eat and defecate at the same time.

Munching on the hay will stimulate your guinea pig's digestive system and may cause him to use the box, as you intended. If your guinea pig prefers to sleep in his litter box rather than use it as a toilet, you may want to provide him with a more attractive bed than he has. Try using a different bedding material.

Once your guinea pig appears to be using the litter box in his cage and has been allowed to do so for some time, you can try giving him a little more space.

Create a special part of the house just for him. (Kitchens, bathrooms, or hallways work best.) Use a baby gate to section off a small area to keep an eye on him.

Place the litter box in the small room, along with the guinea pig's food, water, and bedding. Watch your guinea pig; make sure he uses the litter box regularly.

If he uses the litter box successfully, you can increase the amount of space in the house accessible to him.

If your guinea pig starts making mistakes at any point in the process, it might have been too early to put him in a bigger location. Return him to his cage and start over. Or you may want to try buying a few more litter boxes and placing them in various parts of the guinea pig's space. With several litter box choices to choose from, he is more likely to get the right idea.

Understand that your guinea pig may never learn to use the litter box reliably and will more than likely have occasional accidents. Patience, understanding, and a sense of humor will help you cope with this situation. Try to come up with ideas on how to adapt to your guinea pig's bathroom habits.

CHAPTER 5

UNDERSTANDING SOME COMMON BEHAVIORS IN GUINEA PIG

GUINEA PIG SOUNDS

Guinea pigs produce some sounds or vocalizations which would be heard by most owners. Contented guinea pigs also make some squeaks, chortles, and quiet grunts, which often seem to accompany casual interactions. With these repeated squeaks and chortles, you may hear from your guinea pig some other very distinctive noises. Learn to learn these!

Guinea pigs don't talk (be very afraid if you find one that does!), but just because they don't have actual conversations with their owners doesn't mean that they don't know how to communicate. Sounds, along with their body movements, are made by cavies to communicate to their owners and other cavies. This chapter serves as a guide that you can use to decipher the sounds made by your pet.

Wheeking:

Wheeking is used to describe the whistling sounds your pets may make. There are different kinds of wheeking, which pertain to different emotions, and these are:

High-pitched tones. High-pitched whistles are usually made by pups when they are separated from their mothers.

High, rising tones. High whistling notes indicate that your cavies are excited. These usually make these sounds if they're hungry and are about to be fed.

Level tones. Level whistling sounds are usually made by one cavy when they encounter another cavy. They sometimes make this sound if they think they're lost.

Low tones. If the whistling sounds your furry companion makes are low and distinctly grumpy-sounding, it means your pet isn't in a good mood and doesn't want to get touched by or play with you.

Purring:

Purring usually denotes contentment and calmness. They usually do this after being fed or while they're being stroked. However, a high-pitched purring sound can also indicate that your guinea pig is tense or annoyed. The sound made when the cavy is enjoying itself/being happy (e.g., when being petted or held). Sound can also be produced when given food, grooming, or crawling around to investigate a new place

NOTE: Beware of the purring pitch and body language which complements this sound category and could change the original meaning (if the purr is higher-pitched toward the end, and the cavy seems to vibrate and tense, this could be interpreted as a sound of annoyance).

Rumbling:

Rumbling can be distinguished from purring if you feel or see that your guinea pig is vibrating while making this sound. These guinea pig sounds are reserved for the mating purpose, with males usually doing this to romance females. Rumbling sounds may be made while your pets are doing a mating dance.

A boar may also rumble to show its dominance within a group of cavies. Response to being scared or angry in which case the rumble often sounds higher, and the body vibrates shortly also related to dominance within a group. Petting in the wrong spots (for instance, on cavy's underside) often results in low rumbling sound.

Chattering:

Guinea pigs make their teeth chatter when they're agitated or angry. If they show their teeth while making these sounds, watch out, because it's their way of telling you to back off. Chattering noises may also be accompanied by hissing, which denotes the same thing. On the other hand, a relaxed, chattering sound could indicate that your pet is hungry and begging for treats.

Aggressive vocalization: a sign of an agitated or angry cavy sound is made by rapidly gnashing the teeth often accompanied by showing the teeth (looks like a yawn, but more sinister) and raising the head freely interpreted as "back off" or "stay away."

Cooing:

A mother usually coos to their babies to reassure them of their presence.

Shrieking:

Believe it or not, guinea pigs can scream! Shrieking indicates fear, alarm, or pain. Be sure to check up on your pets when they make this noise, as one of them could be hurt.

A high-pitched sound of discontent, pain and fear

Response to pain or immediate danger

! URGENT NOTE: Check on your cavy ASAP to make sure everything is okay!

Whining:

A whining or moaning type of squeak can communicate annoyance or dislike for something you or another guinea pig is doing.

Used to communicate annoyance or dislike for something an owner or another cavy is doing can be head in pursuit situations (both the pursuer and the pursuee).

Chirping:

Cavies can also make the same chirping sounds as birds make. This is one of the least-understood guinea pig sounds, although some people postulate that it's the sound babies make when they want to be fed by their mothers.

Possibly the least understood or heard a noise a sound patterns similar to bird song

Could be related to stress or when baby pigs want to be fed.

SLEEPING HABIT

Guinea pigs do not need long periods of sleep because they are not nocturnal animals such as hamsters. During daytime and night, they have to take small naps. A Guinea pig will usually relax and rest their head on the ground, and some of them will be relaxed and spread their hind legs.

POPCORNING

Most owners consider popcorning as the most interesting aspect of guinea pig behavior. This refers to the event when cavies suddenly start leaping in the air. Young guinea pigs usually jump straight up as if they were wearing pogo sticks.

When cavies engage in this behavior, they are trying to show you that they are very happy and content with their lives. Since only healthy cavies exhibit this behavior, you have the right to swell with pride every time your critters start leaping to the air.

Why Do Guinea Pigs Popcorn?

To show absolute joy and enthusiasm, Guinea pigs popcorn (mainly) It is a completely natural activity you will see from time to time most guinea pigs waking up. However, it should be remembered that not all the guinea pigs popcorn and that as long as you have the following, you shouldn't worry they don't.

- A healthy diet
- Clean water
- Daily playtime
- Interaction with yourself

You should also remember that a Guinea pig can sometimes popcorn out of fear. It's critical to pay attention to the circumstances where your guinea pig is popcorning. If the popping can appear to be fear-based, you should locate the trigger and eliminate it.

Can I Get My Guinea Pig to Popcorn?

Sure, you can, and the best way to do that is to give them stuff you know they want. Providing joy and enjoyment, after all, is the way into the heart of a guinea pig.

Tasty Treats- Because you probably already know guinea pigs enjoy their fruit treats and veggie treats and feeding them some is a perfect way to make them popcorn. Though, you should be careful not to overdo it because too much of a good thing can cause diarrhea.

Several people have even mentioned bringing their guinea pig to popcorn on cue. We did that by saying words like pop while they were giving them a treat. In effect, the guinea pig has eventually associated popcorning with the title, and they'll pop on cue 'hey presto.'

New Toys- Guinea pigs enjoy only their toys. They enrich their daily lives, and there is always a new one that will drum up excitement. Tunnels, bins, ladders, or sticks, it doesn't matter, guinea pigs will popcorn to all of them. You may want to try to change your guinea pigs' toys regularly, so they always feel like a fresh and exciting (popcorning) experience.

Play with Your Guinea Pig- Giving your guinea pig time off their cage to play, and with you is a perfect way to motivate them to popcorn. Also, it is always the best approach and the most efficient. You can also pick up, hold, and pet your guinea pig by treating them to popcorn when you put them back in their cage.

DOMINANCE

What is Guinea Pig Dominance?

The behavior of dominance does not mean that even two guinea pigs cannot share the same cage. It just means that one of them, particularly if they were the first to have the cage, will mark his / her territory. They'll try to convince the younger guinea pig that they're the boss and they'll live together happily as soon as the new one catches on.

The dominant behavior in guinea pigs is distinct from their cycle of bonding and depends on each person and the circumstances surrounding that behavior. This conduct generally isn't that insane and won't need your interference. But if this cycle is too intense and starts to include fights or aggression, you should try to isolate them. But you can never separate them if they usually seek to develop dominance.

And it's really important that you know the difference between whether they're either playing or battling around.

Guinea Pig Dominance Behavior

Dominance varies from one guinea pig to another and their different circumstances. The chattering of teeth is one of the most common behaviors. This generally means they are not pleased with the situation they find themselves in. Once you introduce a new addition to the cage, you can find them doing that immediately.

The move is meant to frighten the newcomers into submission. All guinea pig's will chatter teeth, so it shouldn't bother you when both do.

Another common conduct is humping. The dominant guinea pig usually mounts the one they want to overwhelm. Mounting is never romantic and shouldn't make you fear. It means they seek to mark their territories by showing the weaker one they have.

For guinea pigs, this action may also mean that the dominant one shows the dominant partner that they are on top. With this action of superiority, their gender, and relationship to each other generally don't matter. A male can climb onto another male even if it's connected just to show they're stronger.

GROOMING EACH OTHER

Why guinea pigs groom

If you've got pet guinea pigs, you have to remember they're attentive groomers.

As well as brushing their cage mates and human partner, Guinea pigs. Some can groom styles prevalent in guinea pigs are:

Self-grooming: This is when guinea pigs groom themselves.

All grooming: It is when two or more guinea pigs groom each other.

Social grooming: This is when guinea pigs try to groom their owner or human companion.

But why do guinea pigs take grooming seriously?

Safety: Guinea pigs are prey species, and from predators, they need to stay incognito. Grooming plays a crucial role in neutralizing the smell and safeguarding it from predators.

Maintaining Body Temperature: Guinea pigs don't sweat. Which means guinea pigs need to clean themselves in hot weather conditions to keep their body cool.

Shedding: Grooming also allows the body to rid itself of any excess hair. It is key to maintaining control of their body temperature.

Reducing Stress: Grooming is also effective in keeping the guinea pigs self-sufficient. To raising their tension, they groom themselves.

Love and Affection: Guinea pigs do groom their companion to share their passion and affection. This can be compared to a hug.

Dominance or Hierarchy: Grooming in the cage is also useful in maintaining dominance or hierarchy. The subordinate guinea pig should allow the daily grooming of the dominant guinea pig.

Grooming is an integral part of the routine for the guinea pig. If your guinea pig doesn't groom properly, then it could be a sign of a medical concern.

FIGHTING EACH OTHER

Reasons Why Your Guinea Pigs Might Be Fighting

Guinea pigs are friendly and cute, usually relaxed animals in most circumstances. Yet no matter what sort of species we interact with, conflict is bound to be one way or another. Whether its humans, cats, rats, or birds, we all encounter struggle now and then. The real question is, why do guinea pigs fight?

1. Establishing Dominance

Usually, there would be a dominant piggie in a herd of guinea pigs, and you can tell who it is from the way they are fighting. Usually, the last to stand their ground is more dominant. In guinea pig colonies, battling for supremacy is common and is good as long as one guinea pig backs down and behaves submissively towards the other. The real problem is when none of the piggies backs down, and things get more violent. This is when you need to step in and stop the fight.

2. Physical Pain/Illness

Guinea pigs are typically very friendly pets that work together well if matched properly. When one of your guinea pigs starts behaving out of the blue, they could be experiencing pain in their body somewhere.

Like any other person or pet, it may lead to an angry and cranky disposition to feel ill or pain. Make sure your piggie is checked and taken to a vet just to be healthy. Please try to feed their cage properly and disinfect it to avoid getting any of your guinea pigs sick.

3. Pairing

Pairing guinea pigs properly is a vital job to keep things in your guinea pig kingdom happy. This should be advised that males and females be kept apart. Mixing the two guinea pig genders can lead to mating fights. Another way of matching a guinea pig is by adding it to a younger one. The guinea pigs thus establish dominance much more quickly.

4. Small Cage

When multiple piggies are put in a small, cramped room, they are naturally going to start having problems! There is nowhere for one to get away from the other, with a little freedom to play. If they're too long trapped together, they'll start getting mad at each other and start a fight.

Cages would also allow all the guinea pigs plenty of room to hide in. If you have just one hidey, then put a pocket liner down for the other to rest in. This way, they can have some privacy among themselves.

5. Boredom/Unhappiness

They get bored and frustrated when you aren't enticing your guinea pig with toys, vegetables, or anything. Which means they will have a greater chance to start a war with other piggies.

Make sure they have plenty to do to stop this. It can be as easy as humming on hay or letting them out for floor time, just make sure there's plenty of fun going around there. Therefore, not all fights necessarily require attention. Many fights occur when there is no real problem present and will most likely finish faster than anticipated. Only watch as combat gets more serious, and be prepared to stop it.

HIDING

Mechanism of natural protection that needs to be valued and treated patiently. When you follow the Guinea Pig Book guidelines, it does not need to be perceived as a denial or its creator. These are some of the reasons why your Guinea hide and how you can help them to overcome home

Potential danger

Guinea pigs are always alert from potential threats, and if they feel insecure in any way, then they will run for their life.

The only defense that our guinea pigs have against potential risks is running away and hiding.

Look out for something in their living space that might be frightening them and get rid of the same.

Some common problems include your other household pets like birds, cats, dogs, etc. Sometimes kids or any visitors whom your guinea pigs are not accustomed to can also frighten them out.

So, make sure you never let any visitors handle your guinea pigs or chase them around their cage as it can stress them out.

You must provide them a sense of security so that they can relax and come out more often.

Shy in nature

Every guinea pig is different, and some guinea pigs do have a shy nature. If your guinea pig is one of them who has a shy nature, then you must give them some time to get used to things around them.

Many owners see that their friend is cuddling and playing with their guinea pigs, and they think that they will also do the same.

However, there is a possibility that your guinea pigs might not allow you to do so. Some guinea pigs even refuse to come out of their hiding when someone is around them. This is their nature, and we have to work around it.

Scared of owners

Guinea pigs can get scared pretty easily, and if you have just brought your new guinea pig home, then chances are they are scared of you, and they will not come out when you are around.

You need to introduce yourself slowly to them so that they can get used to you. Sometimes our sudden movement can frighten them. Some guinea pig owners also try to sneak up on their guinea pigs, but I would caution you not to do so.

Doing so can result in loss of trust, and your guinea pigs might take even longer to get accustomed to your presence.

You should instead not try to touch them or handle them much when you first get them. Let them get used to their environment so they can come out more often.

Also, if you have kids in your home, you must not allow them to play or handle your guinea pigs in those early days.

It is essential to introduce your guinea pigs slowly to everyone. They may get overwhelmed if all of your family members get around your guinea pigs.

Sudden loud noises

Guinea pigs don't like loud noises, and any sudden loud noise like a thunderstorm, firecrackers, a passing dumpster truck, etc. can frighten your guinea pigs.

A frightened guinea pig will run for their lives and hide until they feel safe. So, if your guinea pig is hiding whenever there is a loud noise around them, then it is entirely normal and part of their natural behavior.

Sometimes loud music and television can also frighten your guinea pigs. Thus, it is recommended to avoid such noises around them.

It is also seen that extended exposure to loud noises can cause some severe health issues in guinea pigs as well. You can always play soft music around if your guinea pigs enjoy them but avoid any loud sounds.

Keeping a single guinea pigs

Guinea pigs are herd animals, and they do need a company to live a long and happy life. If you are keeping a single guinea pig, then chances are they are feeling lonely, lethargic, or maybe even depressed.

Guinea pigs with such symptoms tend to hide all the time and are less active than other guinea pigs.

Some owners say that they provide them with enough floortime and toys to play with, but the reality is it is tough to provide them with interaction, vocalization, and bond that two guinea pigs share.

Thus, your guinea pig may be hiding all the time because they are feeling lonely and depressed.

Sleeping

Guinea pigs are always alert, and they won't sleep with their eyes closed until they feel secure. You will notice that your guinea pig is hiding and taking a nap, and it is entirely normal for them.

Guinea pigs usually like to get into a comfortable hiding place and take a short nap because they feel much more secure that way.

If your guinea pig is closing their eyes well sleeping, then you should be more than happy as it means they feel content and safe in their living space.

Health problems

Health problems are not rare in guinea pigs. However, guinea pigs are known to hide their health problems until it gets severe.

This can be a big concern for beginners as they can't understand what is wrong with their guinea pigs.

Some guinea pigs also hide all the time and will not even come out for eating, and if you see something similar in your guinea pigs, then you must understand that there is a possible health problem in your guinea pigs.

You must look out for other symptoms of health problems and reach out to a vet immediately if you notice anything like this.

Some of the common health problems include dental problems, Respiratory problems, and Gastrointestinal problems.

Most of these will require professional help. Thus, it is recommended to avoid trying any home remedies and approach a vet.

How do I stop my guinea pig from hiding?

To get your guinea pigs out from the hiding, you must first understand why is your guinea pig hiding?

Once you have figured out the right cause, you can take appropriate action to get them out. Let us have a look at some possible solutions to get your guinea pigs out from the hiding.

Well maintained living environment

Providing your guinea pigs with an appropriate living space that has food, water, and other essential supplies is crucial.

Once your guinea pig feels like home, they are more likely to explore their living environment. Make sure the living environment is clean and safe for your guinea pigs.

Also, place the cage at the central part of your home where heat and cold waves don't affect them much. Avoid loud noises, kitchen fumes, and other strong smells around your guinea pig's living space.

These can easily stress them out, and as a result, your guinea pigs are more likely to remain inside hiding.

Hand feeding your guinea pigs

The way to your guinea pig's heart goes through their stomach. Although this may sound a little cheesy, but it is a fact that guinea pig associates good things with food.

This means if you feed them veggies or treats like carrots, watermelon, pea flakes, etc. then they will get used to you quickly.

Hand Feeding your guinea pigs also builds a strong bond with them, and they are more likely to come out and wheek and play with you rather than hiding when you are around.

However, don't overfeed them with treats as they are bad for their health in the long-run. You can start with some treats and replace them with veggies as your guinea pigs get accustomed to it.

Provide more floortime

Guinea pigs are active animals, and they do need a lot of space to eat, play, and exercise. If your cage doesn't provide them with enough space, then you must consider providing them with some floortime.

Floortime not only makes them active but also allows them to interact with new elements in their environment. It is also helpful in the introduction of other family members or friends during the process, which makes them less likely to hide in the foreseeable future.

Apart from that, your guinea pigs will also remain healthy and active if they are provided enough space and time to play and exercise.

Don't chase them around to catch them

Guinea pigs are fluffy and cute little pets, and often their owners want to cuddle and pet them.

However, not all guinea pigs enjoy the same. Sometimes a new owner tries to hold them, and when guinea pigs are not willing to come on their own, they chase them around to get a hold of them.

Doing so can stress your guinea pigs out, and you will lose the trust you are trying to build. Thus, you should never chase your guinea pigs around the cage to get a hold of them.

Instead, it should be the other way around. Offer some attractive treats and snacks from your hand by keeping a distance. Let your guinea pigs come towards you and never try to chase them around.

Have patience

Guinea pigs make a lovely pet if you take good care of them and have some patience while training them. Not all guinea pigs carry the same nature; thus, it is crucial to understand the nature of your guinea pigs and give them time to adjust to their environment and your presence.

If you try to rush things, then it can be challenging to develop a good bond between you and your guinea pigs. Patience is the key when it comes to building a bond and training your pets.

Have patience, make a good bond with your pet, and provide them with adequate living space, and your guinea pigs will be around you all the time.

Guinea pigs only run away and hide when they see you as a threat. So, building a good bond is the key to fix the problem for once and all.

Get a pair of guinea pigs or more

Guinea pigs are social animals, and they do enjoy living in a group of two or more. Getting a single guinea pig can be a bad idea, primarily if you cannot provide enough attention to them.

In most scenarios, having more than one guinea pig is ideal. When kept in groups, your guinea pigs will remain active and happy, and thus they will not hide anymore.

Occasional nap or games around their hiding is usual. Still, if you feel your guinea pig is lonely and not active, then probably they need a partner, and getting them a good partner will encourage them to come out and play and exercise.

Visiting a vet

Guinea pigs are known for hiding their health problems, and so it is crucial to visit a professional vet who can look out for signs of those issues and treat them accordingly.

Guinea pigs are fragile creatures when it comes to their health. Their health can go from good to bad in a matter of 24-48 hours.

So, paying close attention to their health and reaching out to a vet if you find any health issue is critical.

Sometimes the health issues are not apparent, and you must look out for other signs like loss of appetite, losing weight, lethargy, hiding a lot, etc.

If you see those signs accompanying your guinea pigs, then it is certain that they need medical care immediately.

BITING

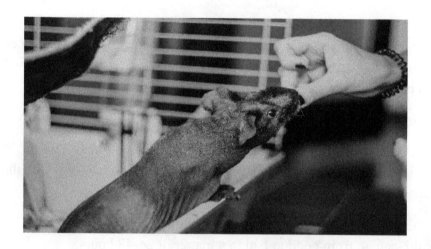

Considered a rare, but not unusual, behavioral pattern. A Guinea pig will bite you for a variety of reasons:

If it is upset, angry, frightened, defensive, or annoyed.

Maybe the result of an accident; if you've been handling food, for example, the guinea pig may make the mistake of believing that your finger is food. It's recommended that you wash your hands to avoid such errors and keep your fingers.

They can bite because of a skin problem like mites, and it can cause extreme discomfort to hold, stroke, or touch a guinea pig with mites, and they will do anything to stop the pain.

CHAPTER 6

FEEDING YOUR GUINEA PIG

The way you feed your guinea pig will mean the difference between a good, long-lived pet and a sickly, unhappy animal. Guinea pigs are herbivores, and in the wild, they are animals who spend considerable amounts of time foraging for and eating plants. Since plant content is difficult to break down, the guinea pig's digestive system is somewhat different from that of carnivores (like cats) and omnivores (like us).

It's important to give your guinea pig a diet that simulates the diet she would eat in the wild. Failure to do so will result in a guinea pig with chronic diarrhea, heart, liver, and kidney disease, and obesity.

Hay

When you bought your guinea pigs cage or hutch, you even purchased a hay rack. Guinea pigs need free access to fibrous foods, and hay, which is pure roughage, suits the bill. Hay can be purchased from various outlets, including pet supply shops, feed shops, and local horse stables. When you buy hay, check it for freshness.

Nice, clean hay should have a sweet scent and minimal dust. Examine it for mold, which can be very dangerous to guinea pigs if swallowed. Do not buy hay that is wet or damp. Once you get it in, store the hay in a cool position safe from rain or dampness.

You'll find a variety of hay to choose from. Your pet supply store will stock packaged alfalfa and timothy hay, while feed stores and stables will have baled hay. Timothy hay is generally the best. If your guinea pig is eating pellets, alfalfa hay is already included in her diet. The addition of more alfalfa may cause her to become overweight. (Hay cubes, designed for horses, are not approved for guinea pigs.)

Give your guinea pig a handful of fresh hay to keep her digestive system in working order. Place the hay in the hay rack to help prevent it from flying across the pen. Remove old hay from the cage and the rack before you replace it with new hay.

VEGGIES

Pellets and hay should not be the only foods your guinea pig needs. Fresh greens are also an essential part of her diet and should be provided every day. Some of the best fresh foods for guinea pigs include dark green vegetables such as romaine lettuce, dandelion greens, carrot tops, broccoli, basil, spinach, and artichokes.

Many other leafy green vegetables that humans eat are good for guinea pigs, too, provided the leaves are dark green. Dark green leaves provide your guinea pig with valuable vitamin C, which she cannot manufacture independently.

Ensure sure the vegetables you give your guinea pig are new. Purchase them from the produce section of your supermarket, from a natural food shop, or a farm stand, and make sure to wash them thoroughly.

Do not gather greens form fields unless you can be completely certain the plants have not been sprayed with chemicals and that they are not poisonous. If you can find them, organically grown greens are by far the best option for guinea pigs.

Feeding your guinea pigs

Feed each guinea pig approximately I cup of fresh vegetables daily

Daily

Greens	Other Vegetables
Butterhead Lettuce	Bell pepper (Green, Yellow)
Endive	Tomatoes (Red, Grape or Cherry)
Escarole	
Green Leaf Lettuce	
Radicchio	
Red Leaf Lettuce	

1-2 times per week

Greens	Other Vegetables
Collard Greens	Asparagus
Dill	Basil
Kate	Beets
Spinach	Broccoli
Turnip Greens	Brussels spouts
Watercress	Cauliflower
	Ram Pumpkin (No Seeds)

2-4 times per week

Greens	Other Vegetables
Arugula	Baby Carrot (1 per guinea pig on a treat)
Broccoli Leaves	Beans (Snap, Green)
Chicory Greens	Bell Pepper (Red)
Dandelion Greens	Celery (cut into small pieces and remove strings)

Mustard Greens	Corn Husk and Silks
Parsley	Cucumber (with peel)
Romaine Lettuce	Peas (in the pod)
Thyme	Squash (summer of winter)
	Turnips

Fruit

In common language usage, "fruit" means the fleshy seed-mix structures of a plant that are sour or sweet, and edible in the raw state, such as bananas, apples, lemons, oranges, grapes and strawberries. On the other hand, in botanical usage, "fruit" includes many structures that are not commonly called "fruits", such as bean pods, corn kernels, tomatoes, and wheat grains. The section of a fungus that produces spores is also called a fruiting body.

Feed once per week or twice per week and in a small amount as special treats

Apple (with Skin; Care and Seeds Removed)	Orange (with peel)
Blackberries	Peach
Blueberries	Pear
Grapes (Red, or Green; Seedles)	Pineapple
Kiwi	Plum
Mango	Rasberries
Melon	Strawberries
Cantoloupe	Watermelon (with Rind)

Feeding tips

- About 20 strip of cilantro and a 1/8 bell pepper (red, yellow or green) slice per guinea pigue are good daily staples to ensure vitamin C intake.
- Guinea pigs are grazing animals, consider separating daily vegetables into two meals, each at morning and evening when guinea pig is at most active.
- If you don't know if a vegetable is safe to feed, don't feed it.

PELLETS

People tend to assume that pelleted foods as something only rabbits consume, but specially made pellets only for guinea pigs are the mainstay of a safe guinea pig's diet. When combined with fresh foods, these pellets provide good meals for the guinea pig.

Unlike most other animals, Guinea pigs are unable to produce vitamin C in their bodies and also need a lot of folic acids, so it is necessary to feed them with pellets made specifically for guinea pigs because these pellets contain certain nutrients.

When you buy a pellet guinea pig food, look for a product that contains at least 8 percent protein, 16 percent fiber, and 1 gram of vitamin C / kilogram. Scan the packaging to make sure the pellets are labeled as nutritionally full.

Stop foods that contain animal products, beet pulp, corn products, seeds, nuts, fats, dietary fiber, rice bran, and rice flour. Additives such as corn syrup, sucrose, propylene glycol, food colorings, propyl gallate, potassium sorbate, sodium nitrate, sodium nitrite, sodium metabisulfite, ethoxyquin, and butylated hydroxyanisole should also be avoided.

Please do not buy a large supply of pellets, because they will lose their nutritional value over time. Get the same in a month or so as your guinea pig would feed in. Store the food in the refrigerator, where it will stay fresher longer.

If your guinea pig is younger than three months old, you may leave a bowl of pellets in her cage to eat whenever she wishes. However, if you have an adult, you can have two servings of two tablespoons per day. Feeding the animal once in the morning and once in the evening is ideal. If the guinea pig continues to get fat, you will have to cut down to one tablespoon a day.

You may also want to try our workout time. If your guinea pig does not eat all the pellets, you place in her dish, throw the old ones away before you refill the bowl. It's essential to give only fresh pellets.

TREATS

Guinea pigs enjoy getting daily treats. Feeding her treats will help the two of you bond and will complement her diet. The healthiest foods to feed your guinea pig are new fruits. Some that guinea pigs enjoy include oranges, apples, pears, strawberries, peaches, melons, and tomatoes.

Although these items are particularly popular among guinea pigs, you can give your pet just about any fruit. Just be sure to feed in moderation. (Carrots, though not a fruit, are also a guinea pig favorite.)

Commercially made treats can also be suitable for guinea pigs, as long as you don't overfeed. Stop offering your guinea pig commercial treats that contain sugar or dairy products. It's also prudent to refrain from giving your pet conventional human treats that are high in sugar or salt, including sweets and chocolate.

Occasionally, you may even want to give your guinea pig some dried and aged twigs from an unsprayed fruit tree as a treat. Guinea pigs love to gnaw on trees and occasionally tear off the bark and eat it. (Drying and aging are important since some tree branches are poisonous when fresh.)

GROWING A GUINEA PIG GARDEN

Y̶ou may also want to consider growing a garden for your guinea pig, where she can forage greens as nature intended. Good garden plants that are healthy for guinea pigs include coltsfoot, dandelions, deadnettles, ground elder, mugwort, ragwort, shepherd's purse, and yarrow. Guinea pigs also like to nibble on Bermuda grass and clover.

To create a guinea pig garden, set aside a patch of your backyard for your pet's plants. Be sure to use organic soil and no pesticides or chemical fertilizers. When the plants are mature, create a protective enclosure for your guinea pig. Then let your guinea pig run loose among the plants to graze to her heart's content.

When you supervise her, you'll have the chance to see your guinea pig's wild side when she indulges her natural browsing instincts. (Many common plants are poisonous, so your pet's foraging should be restricted to plants that are known to be healthy. That includes weeding her garden before you turn her loose.)

If your guinea pig never goes outside, you can grow some of these same plants in a wide tray on your balcony or fire escape, bring the tray inside every so often, and let your guinea pig munch on them. She will love the chance to pick her greens, and you will have fun watching her.

Let your guinea pig visit the garden or tray once or twice a week. On the other days, be sure to provide her with different greens than the ones you are developing, so she can have variety in her diet. When your guinea pig is not used to consuming new foods, add these things slowly to her diet, so she does not get diarrhea.

Start by giving her one new food item once a week. Finally, your guinea pig will be consuming three different forms of fresh greens daily, making up no more than 15 percent of her diet. Ensure to immediately remove uneaten greens from your guinea pig's pen.

You may find that your guinea pig has a sensitivity to a specific vegetable. You'll know because she will get diarrhea not long after she eats it. If this happens, remove the offending food from her diet.

WATER

Water is an essential part of the diet for a Guinea pig. We must always ensure that our Guinea pigs have access to Clean and Fresh drinking water at all times.

How much water does a guinea pig need?

Guinea pigs can consume anywhere between 50ml to over 300ml of water every day. They require fresh and clean water all the time. Although, the amount of water they need does vary for every individual guinea pigs. You should always ensure that your guinea pig has fresh water all the time.

How much water do guinea pigs drink every day?

The consumption of water also depends upon their body weight. Usually, 20% of their weight is the amount of water they consume daily. Both extremes can be just fine as it all depends on one guinea pig to another. The consumption of water by them depends on a lot of factors like:

- Weather conditions
- Indoor heating/cooling.
- Diet etc.

So, it is totally fine even if your Guinea pig is drinking 60-70 ml of water or 300ml of water until and unless that is their regular consumption. But, if you see any significant change in water consumption, then you must immediately try to know the cause of the same and fix it.

Can guinea pigs drink tap water?

I often see people getting confused with whether they should give their guinea pig distilled water, tap water, or any sort of special water made for the rodent. What I have learned is if you give your guinea pig the water you can drink then it's totally fine for them. **You should never give your guinea pig distilled water.** Simple filtered tap water would just be great for them.

Always ensure that the water is free from any sort of chemicals and contamination. It is also essential to provide them with water at room temperature.

Can guinea pigs drink cold water?

You could give them somewhat cold water in scorching summer but try to stick with room temperature on any usual day. You should not provide them with warm water as they refuse to drink that at all.

Your guinea pig must NEVER be fed Alcohol, Aerated water, or anything similar to it. Serving those may lead to fatal health issues or in the worst case, a Life threat for them. Should I add any supplements to the water for my Guinea pigs?

There are a ton of medicines and vitamin supplements that can be added to their water. However, do not add any sort of vitamin additives or minerals in the water because in most cases, they will try to avoid drinking much of it. Avoiding water for long may lead to dehydration in them in the long run.

Adding additives to water also makes them a home for algae, which is a bad thing for your guinea pigs. Also adding any sort of medication to water is a bad idea because you cannot control the intake of water.

Also, most of the medications are really bad in smell and taste so your guinea pig will not even bother going near to it. The guinea pig has double the number of taste buds as compared to humans. So, you cannot fool them that easily.

How should I provide water to my Guinea pig?

Provide your guinea pig with water in a way they are comfortable with, and they can have access to it at all times. There are many different ways to provide them with fresh water, but the choice of it will be dependent upon your guinea pig preference. You need to do some trials and see which system they prefer the most.

Can guinea pigs drink water from Bottles?

The plastic and glass bottles are widely being used all around the world for providing water to the guinea pig. Unfortunately, there is no leak-proof and problem-free bottle available in the world just yet so we must depend upon it in most cases. Both the glass and plastic bottle is clipped from outside the cage with the pipe like nozzle reaching in from which Guinea pigs can sip the water.

Although this is better than bowls as they are less prone to contamination and refilling is quite easy too.

It is preferred to get a glass bottle instead of a plastic one because those are less prone to the algae issue. The room temperature will vastly not impact the water if it's in good glass bottles. Also, the glass bottle has a larger nozzle size, which makes it more comfortable for a guinea pig to use.

But at the same time, plastic bottles are way cheaper than a glass bottle. Although widely used these types of bottles come with a significant disadvantage.

Firstly, it is really tough to create a vacuum so that the bottle doesn't drip or leak. Many people try to fill the bottle till the end so that it doesn't drip, but that is not the right way and in cold regions water may freeze and burst the bottles in some cases.

Secondly, in this type of bottle Guinea pigs must use their tongue to hit the ball in the nozzle so that the water comes out, which makes it difficult to drink much water at once.

Also, they usually drink water after having food, so the pellets or food in their mouth gets stuck in the nozzle and can very often choke it.

Bonus tip

Always have an extra set of bottles because you will need to replace them every 10-12 months as they get worn out over time. It is also healthy to keep changing plastic dishes to prevent health issues.

Can guinea pigs drink water from Sippy Bottles?

Sippy bottles are excellent in comparison to standard bottles for any guinea pig. It is much easier for them to drink water from this type of bottle as they simply need to raise the gib at the nozzle, and a continuous stream of water will start flowing in.

Using sippy bottles will also lead to more water consumption as they need not struggle to do so as in the case of standard bottles. If given a choice any guinea pig will lean towards this bottle more. The build quality of these bottles is excellent as it uses much thicker plastic, making it less prone to algae. This bottle does not work on the principle of vacuum; thus, it is less likely to clog.

Although these bottles also have a disadvantage, sometimes they continue to drip water, and so a drip dish is required below it so it doesn't create a mess.

Can guinea pigs drink water from a bowl?

Bowls are the easiest way to supply water to the guinea pigs. Always remember to use heavy ceramic bowls so that they cannot tip them over. Usually, guinea pigs tend to place their front paws in the bowl while drinking, which can lead to tip over if the dish is unsuitable for them. Younger guinea pigs who haven't yet learned to drink from bottles must be provided with water in a bowl so that they do not suffer.

Also, the bowl makes it easier for them to drink as they can just get the water by dipping the head into it. But for some reason, Guinea pig does not like to drink water from Bowls.

Bowls also have a significant disadvantage that the water is more prone to. The feces and food particles often get dropped in it and make water contaminated. So, it is best to avoid it unless and until necessary. Sometimes when the guinea pig is sick and is unable to drink water from the bottle then they can be given a bowl to drink with.

How can I teach my Guinea pig to drink from the bottle?

In young ages, Guinea pigs tend to drink water from bowls rather than bottles. It is always good to encourage them to drink from bottles as it is more hygienic. Do not worry; they will learn to feed on bottles by watching their parents and elders do the same.

You can encourage this mostly by placing a small ceramic container just below the tip of the bottle. Although you may need to change the water 3-4 times a day because a lot of feces and dirt will get accumulated into it.

After some time, you can place some bits of cucumber on the nozzles or anything else they like just to make them try it. Usually, within a few weeks, your Guinea pigs will get used to it and will start drinking water from it.

Alternatively, you can take the bottle in hand and put some treat in the nozzle and bring it near its mouth to get them started. Do not force this upon your Guinea pig as this may lead to even further worse situations in time to come. You will also stress them out a lot by doing so, which is not what we want to do.

We want positive reinforcement and not the negative one. Please fill fresh and clean water every day in the bottle even if not in use. Not changing the water daily will result in algae formation.

How to place water bottles in Guinea pigs cage?

Although this might look like a fundamental question, it's actually an important one because if your Guinea pig needs to stretch out to reach the water, they will be negatively enforced to drink much.

Also having it too low will make them duck in for it again not something you want. Having the water bottle at the correct height is pretty essential and must be learned by beginners while starting out. Although in general keeping the nozzle at the height of 1-2 inches works excellent, it is vital that you try other possibilities too. As not all guinea pigs are the same.

I would recommend putting 2-3 bottles at a different height and see what works the best for you. Also having multiple bottles helps because if one gets blocked, the other one can be used.

How should I clean the water bottle or bowl of my Guinea pig?

Here you have mostly two methods you can go with. Let's have a look at both of them:

1. Firstly, get a commercial cleaning kit that every pet store supply and use the same to rinse off your bottles and bowls. It's quite simple; Just pour the cleaning agent, take the brush and scrub it off from inside and outside and then rinse it off and it's done.

2. Secondly, the more hygienic and budget-friendly way is to take a bit of uncooked rice and some water in the bottle. Now, place a finger in the lid/opening to close it off and shake vigorously. Then empty your dish, and it's spotless!

Always rinse the nozzle too as it contains the most amount of dirt and leftovers. Use a cotton bud by dampening it to clear the ball nozzle.

Always use a baby bottle disinfectant to clean the bottle once in a week or so. It's imperative to provide your Guinea pigs with fresh and clean water.

How can I monitor the amount of water my guinea pigs are drinking?

The most natural way to do so is by using a bottle to feed them the water. In most situations, your pet water consumption will remain consistent. Although weather change and temperature may bring a small change gradually. If you refill the container daily on a schedule, you will be able to monitor the water consumption of your Guinea pig.

It is crucial you follow this quite closely as any significant change in water consumption is the starting sign of sickness in a Guinea pig. If you find your Guinea pig has a substantial change in water consumption, then it's best to give a visit to the vet.

Is my guinea pig drinking too much water?

The ideal consumption of water by a guinea pig is usually 20% of its body weight. Now, this may depend from pig to pig. Some drink around 50-60 ml a day while some drink 200-300 ml. It is quite okay if the consumption is not unusual. But sometimes there are notable changes in water consumption. If your guinea pig is drinking too much water it may be because of the following reasons: -

- If you change the diet of your guinea pig, it may trigger some unusual behavior. Sometimes a change in diet can lead to more water consumption than earlier.
- If you serve more veggies rich in the water earlier, then a change in that can cause more water intake. The same way more hay consumption increases water intake.
- Change in temperature can also sometimes trigger some change. If there is a change in temperature, then it might be the reason for more water consumption. As heat increases the need for water usually goes up too.
- Sometimes dental issues, Bladder stones, urinary tract infections, etc. may also lead to more consumption of water.
- Diabetes is also a reason that increases water intake. You need to do the blood test for detecting the same in your guinea pigs.

Major health issues like kidney failure and digestive disorder can also lead to an increase in water intake.

If there is a notable increase in water consumption of your guinea pig and you are unable to figure out the reason, then it's best to take them to a vet soon. You could wait for a day or two and keep a close eye on any other health issue symptoms. But the best would be to take them to the vet as soon as possible.

Is my Guinea pig drinking too little water?

Sometimes we feel that our pet might be drinking too little water. But that can be due to many reasons. Sometimes it's a regular change whereas sometimes a serious one. Here are the few things to notice if your guinea pig is drinking less water than usual: -

- If there is a change in the diet mostly to more veggies and fruits, then it can lead to less water consumption.

- In a cold environment, water consumption usually goes down.

The taste of water is changed either due to some chemicals like chlorine etc. or due to added supplement by you, which is a common issue that leads to less water consumption.

Sometimes diseases like Mouth infection, Overgrown teeth, Pneumonia, or respiratory problems can also lead to less water consumption. Again, I would suggest taking them to the vet if you are unable to understand the cause. In the meantime, provide them with water-rich veggies like cucumber, celery will fulfill their hydration needs.

What are the symptoms of Dehydration in Guinea pigs?

It might be really tough for a beginner to understand if its pig is dehydrated or not. Unlike other pets, guinea pigs are really good at hiding their illness. So, you must keep a close eye on these signs to detect if something is wrong or not.

Keep a close eye on their pee (stool) color and smell. Generally, the stool color changes dark orange or brown and smells strong when they are dehydrated. You must look closely in their mouth gums. If the gums are dry then its clear sign of dehydration

Check if your Guinea pig is not as active as usual and have been not interacting much then this might also be the reason. Check whether the poop shape is as usual or not. Checking the poop also helps us in understanding many things. Dry and small dropping are the signs of a dehydrated body. Look at their eyes up close. If you see dry eyes, sunken eyes then this may also be the cause of dehydration.

How long can guinea pigs go without water?

A Guinea pig can live up to 8-12 hours without water. But sometimes they are seen living up to 48 hours provided it has enough vegetables to eat. Most of the water requirement of guinea pigs tends to be fulfilled by fresh veggies. So, if you feed them a lot of veggies rich in the water they can live for a day or two without water too.

Although we recommend having access to fresh and clean water all the time. If a guinea pig doesn't have enough water to drink for more than a day, it might lead to dehydration and liver problems in them. Also eating hay makes them thirstier, so if only a hay-based diet is served to them with no water, then it may lead to a severe situation.

Should I Buy Filtered or low calcium water for my Guinea pigs?

If you live in an area where there is hard water coming in your tap Maybe, then you must consider giving your Guinea pig filtered water. Many people don't realize that most of the calcium in the diet of Guinea pigs comes from water and not only pellets and veggies.

Providing your guinea pig with water rich in calcium can lead to diseases like Bladder stones or sludge. You must always test your water before you start serving it to your Guinea pigs.

Some people also tend to buy bottled water for guinea pigs without realizing that unlike said those bottles have high calcium content. It is best recommended to serve your Guinea pig with filtered water to avoid any possible health issues.

Is adding sugar or honey in the water of my Guinea pig safe?

From what I have learned, sugar is not beneficial to anyone. Some beginners try to put some sugar or honey in the water of Guinea pigs just because they think it will increase the water consumption. Maybe it can do so but it's absolutely not recommended at all. Introducing sugar or honey to the diet of a Guinea pig is equal to inviting a bunch of health problems with it.

You can alternatively use some treats like cucumber pieces etc. in a water bottle nozzle to do so. Never ever try to use Sugar just to increase the water consumption of your Guinea pigs.

Will my Guinea pig drink more water if I put hay in it?

Putting hay in the water is a bad idea. Firstly, the hay will go moldy when you put it in water or moist.

Secondly, when the guinea pigs try to dip their mouth into the water bowl to eat hay, they may end up with water in their lungs from the nostrils.

This will further lead to health issues like Pneumonia. The best way is to put a lot of dry hay and Feed them a lot of hay. Eating dry hay will make them thirsty and thus drink more water eventually. You can also feed your Guinea pigs with the right number of veggies that will also fulfill the need of water in their body.

My Guinea pig is not drinking water at all. What should I do?

Sometimes it is quite natural for a guinea pig not to drink water at all. If you have fed him some good fresh veggies like cucumber etc. which have a high degree of fluids, it will fulfill its water needs.

You may notice whenever their vegetable intake goes up, their fluid needs to go down. This is quite natural and you should not worry much about such a case. But, if you find some sudden changes in water intake without any change in diet, then you must look deeply.

If your Guinea pig is less active than usual, have its eyes closed more, if it is not responding well and also their diet has changed, then something surely is going wrong. If any of the above symptoms are seen, you must visit your vet as early as possible.

Sometimes if a Guinea pig is not drinking water then it could also be because of these reasons: -

- The water bottle nozzle is clogged up with some uneaten food or any other particles. And they are unable to actually drink from it.
- The water contains more chlorine or some chemical which is causing the issue.
- The bottle is not clean properly, leading to poor water quality thus avoiding the water.

Some quick tips you can try if you see the problem persist: -

- Clean the water bottle properly at least twice a week and change it if necessary.

- Check if the nozzle is blocked and clean it with a soft cotton bud.
- Serve only filtered water that is free from any chemical or additives.
- If you are too worried, serve them more of fluid rich vegetables like cucumber and celery. Eating these veggies will prevent dehydration for some time.
- Rush to a vet as soon as possible in case the problem lasts for more than a day.

Cecotropes

Some decades ago, researchers found that certain small mammals had an odd way of supplementing their diets. Small, soft pellets known as cecotropes are formed by the guinea pigs cecum (a part of the large intestine).

These cecotropes, which contain different nutrients, move from the anus, and are naturally consumed by the guinea pig. Although this may sound very strange to us, nature created this method to help the guinea pig consume nutrients from the hard-to-digest cellulose content found in plants.

For your guinea pig to get the most nutrients from her vegetarian diet, she must be able to eat a sufficient amount of the cecotropes created by her body. Since these pellets are generally eaten just as they leave the anus, you may sometimes see your guinea pig consuming them as they are made. You should not stop her from doing this. She knows the difference between these pellets and her waste materials.

WHAT FOODS ARE TOXIC TO GUINEA PIGS?

There is a wide range of food that guinea pigs cannot eat. Right from various human food to fruits and vegetables, there are a lot of things that you need to keep in mind while feeding a guinea pig. Some of the most common food that is toxic to our guinea pigs includes:

Meat	Milk	Yogurt	Cheese	Cream
Iceberg lettuce	Avocado	Onions	Leeks	Chives
Shallots	Garlic	Avocado	Lentils	Anything with glue, varnish, dyes, etc.
Nuts & Seeds	Salt	Chocolate	Branches and Stems(except few)	Amaranth Leaves
Bitter melon	Broad beans	Cassava	Soybeans	Fiddlehead
Ginger	Wasabi	Potatoes	Tomatillo	Coconut
Date Fruit	Jackfruit	Olives	Plantain	Prunes
Rhubarb	Mamey Sapote	Sour sop	Tamarind	Vanilla Bean
Juices	Sweets	Pickles	Cooked food	Food meant other animals

Dairy Products: Avoid dairy products like curd, milk, cheese, etc as it can lead to digestive problems in guinea pigs.

Avocado: Avocado contains a lot of fat in it. It also contains a fatty acid like a chemical called persin, which can be harmful to your guinea pig's digestive system.

Coconut: Coconut is another fruit that we should not feed to our guinea pigs. It contains a lot of saturated fat that can have a bad impact on their health. Some guinea pigs are also allergic to coconut.

Alcohol: Alcohol is purely toxic to our guinea pigs. Even a single drop of alcohol can put your guinea pigs in sleep mode forever. Thus, avoid it altogether.

Chocolate: Chocolate is bad for our guinea pigs as guinea pigs cannot digest it well.

Seeds (sunflower, etc): Seeds contain a decent amount of fat in it. Thus, avoid it altogether.

Nuts & dry fruits: Most nuts and dry fruits have some decent amount of sugar and fats in it. Both of these are bad for our guinea pig's health thus it is best to avoid it altogether. They also possess choking hazard in some cases.

Pickles: Pickles contain vinegar and other preservatives which can cause health problems in guinea pigs

Cooked food: Cooked food loses essential vitamins and minerals. It also needs the addition of other ingredients like oil, salt, etc. These ingredients are harmful to our guinea pigs. It can also lead to diarrhea and other health issues.

Fruits and vegetables: Some fruits and vegetables are high in oxalic acids, sugar or some other ingredients that our guinea pigs cannot ingest well. Thus, make sure you avoid it altogether.

Caffeine: Caffeine in the form of tea or coffee is also bad for our guinea pig's health.

Salt: Most salt is made by processing and adding some chemicals into it. They also contain an excessive amount of sodium in it. Thus, avoid salt altogether.

Plantain: It contains a decent amount of sugar in it; thus, it should be avoided at all costs.

CHAPTER 7

GROOMING YOUR GUINEA PIG

One of the primary things you'll see when you begin living with a guinea pig is that he likes grooming himself. Guinea pigs are a lot of like felines in that regard—continually trimming and preparing. Even though your guinea pig grooms himself, he will likewise acknowledge standard grooming from you.

Grooming can help you both bond and will likewise allow you to look your guinea pig over for any symptoms of medical issues.

It's ideal for putting aside one hour every seven days for grooming your shorthaired guinea pig. (Longhaired breeds must be prepped consistently.) Guinea pigs will, in general, shed more at specific periods, and during these shedding periods, it is ideal for brushing your pet no less than one hour every day. In the late-summer, hair starts to drop out in larger amounts than ordinary.

In the winter, the shed hairs are supplanted by more hide to help keep the creature warm. At the point when you are prepared, come up with your grooming apparatuses and locate a good spot where you can sit with your guinea pig on your lap. While you are getting ready to brush him is a decent an ideal opportunity to check his eyes and ears if there is any fluid and inspect under his feet for injuries.

BRUSHING AND COMBING

Start your grooming by brushing your guinea pig. You will see a ton of hair is coming out. One of the thing you will notice when you living with a Guinea pig is that they love grooming their self. Guinea pigs are similar to cat in that aspect, always primping and preening. The fact that Guinea pigs like grooming their self, you still have to help them in grooming, they really appreciate that.

Utilize the brush to smooth and finish in the wake of brushing and for delicate areas, such as the face, ears, stomach, and legs.

When you are brushing and grooming your pet, look out for parasites like lice and vermin.

Lice are little, smoothed bugs, and their essence is normally joined by tingling, scratching, and going bald. Bugs are tiny yet in addition to purpose tingling, balding, and scaly skin. On the off chance that you think there might be lice or bugs on your pet, contact your veterinarian.

They can give you safe prescriptions intended to remove lice and bugs and give you a description of the best way to wipe out these parasites from your guinea pig's body. Never utilize any item made for dogs or cats, as these are excessively poisonous for guinea pigs.

As you broom or brush your guinea pig, look out for any irregularities or wounds on its body that could be signs of sickness or disease. If your guinea pig has long hair, you should utilize your brush to turn out to be any mats you may discover in his jacket.

Give specific consideration to areas in his body where one piece of the body rubs against another, for example, the armpits and crotch. Normally, cautious grooming will keep mats from framing. Another way for longhaired guinea pigs is to cut by an expert custodian who is knowledgeable about dealing with guinea pigs.

TRIMMING TOENAILS

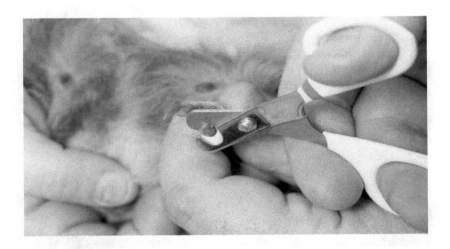

Trimming your guinea pig's toenails is an important piece of your grooming sessions, although it doesn't have to be done weekly.

Check the length and state of your guinea pigs nails each time you groom him. At the point when the nails have all the earmarks of being getting long, the time has come to trim them.

Get ready to trim your guinea pigs nails by putting him tenderly in your lap with his legs upward. Use your scissors to remove a little portion of the nail. Be mindful so as not to cut the snappy (the pink part running inside the focal point of the nail); doing so can hurt the guinea pig and a ridiculous toenail. An outline of the snappy can be seen by holding the nail up to the light.

If you are anxious about trimming your guinea pig's nails for the first time, or if your guinea pig fights back when you attempt to hold him in your lap, you might need to request that your veterinarian tell you the best way to perform this vital part.

BATHING

Even though you may be enticed now and again, make sure you abstain from showering your guinea pig. Are you in doubt, guinea pigs detest being bath and seldom should be, except if they are showed some animals? On the off chance that your guinea pig needs his bottom cleaned, try to clean it with mild soap and water without putting the whole guinea pig in water.

When you have completed, ensure the guinea pig is totally dry before you set him back in his pen, since his wet bottom and feet can draw in egg-laying flies on outdoor guinea pigs or result in sores on the skin.

A shower and a minor trim with scissors at regular intervals may be all together on the off chance that you have a longhaired breed, for example, a Peruvian, Silky, or Texel. You should brush your longhaired pet out cautiously before the shower because any mats or tangles will become like chunks of concrete once they are wet.

You can use a mellow cleanser intended for mutts or cats when bathing your pet and make sure you use heated water. Keep the water in the sink shallow, and use a cup to delicately pour water on your guinea pig to wet his hide. Make sure to flush the cleanser thoroughly out of his jacket. Make sure not to get water in his cavy's ears or eyes. At the point when you need to dry your cavy, put him in a warm, draft free area.

Caress him with a towel. You can likewise blow-dry your guinea pig cavy using a hairdryer on a low setting. Please make sure not to hurt him with the hairdryer, and don't force the issue. The of the hairdryer and its humming might harm him. Just try to make sure he dries naturally.

Grease gland cleaning

In the guinea pig grooming process, cleaning their grease gland is additionally an important advance. Their grease glands are situated in their backs. When you have found their glands, you can look over an assortment of substances in cleaning them. Some people utilize cold-pressed extra virgin coconut oil, Cetaphil, or other gentle purifying substances.

You should make a point to look for guidance from your veterinarian before applying anything into their grease glands. Speedy grease gland checks are a suggested piece of normal consideration and grooming.

While it won't mess up most guinea pigs, a few pigs with extra dynamic grease glands may require help keeping it clean. Letting the gunk persistently develop can cause disturbance and even disease. It's likewise simpler to clean whenever tended to routinely before you will be cleaning a major, clumpy jumble!

Locating where the grease gland is, place your hands down the spine to the tailbone. Around that region, you may discover a detect that is somewhat clingy. This usually occurs; you can use this opportunity to check for any soreness, dry skin, or redness. A filthy grease gland will, in general, appear as though a lot of dim earwax adhered to the hide on the rear end.

Long-haired Guinea pigs may require a little goods trim to make the activity simpler. While a bum shower maybe all together at any rate for those pigs with long, tasty locks, you may find it doesn't completely manage the grease gland goop. A more successful arrangement is to separate the grime with a characteristic degreasing component first.

Coconut oil is a famous, favorite, and protected. Olive oil can likewise work when it's necessary. You may need to let it sit for a piece and even re-do the procedure the next day until some warm water, and a mellow cleanser can complete the activity.

Problems with the Grease gland

Problems with the grease gland don't usually occur but are surely conceivable. If the area is crude, hot to the touch, dying, or is delicate, look for counsel from an expert vet.

A contaminated grease gland should be cleaned expertly before the vet endorses a guinea pig-safe effective and oral anti-infection. In like manner, your vet can help recommend other skin problems, such as parasites or development, or a sebaceous pimple. In case your guinea pig is slanted to problems with the grease gland, talk with your vet about the best way to keep the zone clean at home and forestall rehashing problems.

Shedding

Guinea pigs ordinarily have a great deal of hair, and this shed and re-grows similarly as human hair does. During the springtime, you may see that your guinea pig is shedding considerably more than anticipated. This is normal, as your guinea pig is discarding extra stow away to remain in a very cool way throughout the mid-year.

Much the same as cats and dogs, guinea pigs, or cavies, normally shed their hair so that new hair could grow. This can happen consistently, bringing about a wreck in your pet buddy's living quarters and home. Albeit normal, here and there, shedding may be activated by wellbeing conditions or nourishing inadequacies. To limit the cleanup and keep up a sound, upbeat pet buddy, guarantee he's very much dealt with.

CHAPTER 8

KEEPING YOUR GUINEA PIG HEALTHY

Guinea pigs who are well fed and properly cared for rarely get sick. Nevertheless, if a guinea pig's essential requirements, including a healthy diet, a safe environment, and daily communication and exercise, are not fulfilled, the animal is vulnerable to a variety of harmful illnesses. In other words, taking good care of the guinea pig will result in a healthy pet. Yet, because certain guinea pig diseases are impossible to treat, avoidance is the safest approach.

GUINEA PIG ANATOMY

The body of the guinea pig is the result of her wild ancestors' development and adjustments. Her life structures are intended to assist her with doing her most important assignments: reproducing, eating, and running from predators.

The guinea pig has a short, stocky body, no tail, and huge eyes. The front feet are level, and they normally have four digits with paws. The rear feet have three digits with hooks and are longer than the front feet. Full-developed household guinea pigs weigh somewhere in the range of two and three pounds and measure around ten inches long.

The Coat

A domestic guinea pig arrives in an assortment of colors, on account of specific rearing by people. A common choice did not influence the local guinea pig's shifted examples, except for agouti. Agouti is the Regardless of color, all guinea pigs' coats are comprised of huge, coarse watchman hairs and an undercoat of better hair.

Every hair on the guinea pig's body has a follicle situated close to a sebaceous gland. The guinea pig's sebaceous glands give oil to the skin and coat to keep it solid.

The guinea pig's whole body is secured with hair, aside from her ear folds, the area behind the ear, and the stack of her feet. Five or six rows of bristles are located on each side of the guinea pig's nose.

Bones and Muscles

The guinea pigs skeleton and strong structure give the animal speed for fast excursions and the capacity to eat plants—her common eating diet effectively. The thirty-four vertebrae and thirteen to fourteen ribs give the essential casing of the guinea pig's body.

This edge supports a generally huge skull, which makes up around 33% of the guinea pig's complete bodyweight. The muscles that protect the skeleton are called skeletal muscles. These muscles are what empower the guinea pig to move quickly and do various physical exercises.

The most amazing muscles on the guinea pig's body are the masticator muscles, situated on the jaw. These muscles empower the guinea pig to chew on husks, units, and shells to get to the seeds inside and to crush this extreme food down into fine particles. These are necessities for an animal whose whole eating routine comprises of plant material.

The guinea pig's dentition—twenty teeth altogether—is important to her endurance. She has etched like incisors and rootless molars. All of these teeth keep developing throughout the animal's life to make up for the way they wear out through consistent use.

The guinea pig's gastrointestinal system is designed to digest plant fiber efficiently and can turn 80 percent of the food she consumes into energy. The process starts with the softening of the food in the animal's stomach, from where it travels down into the large intestine.

From there, what has not yet been digested goes to a part of the guinea pig's anatomy called the cecum. Compared to a human appendix, the cecum is on the left side of the guinea pig's body and makes up about 15 percent of the animal's total weight. The cecum's function is to house bacteria that can break down the cellulose in plant matter. This cellulose is converted into digestible carbohydrate constituents.

Until the guinea pig receives the nutrients from the plant matter digested in the cecum, the food content must return to the stomach. It is done by a method called refection. The guinea pig ejects the material in pellet form from her anus and then eats it. Once the pellet gets to the stomach, the carbohydrates are absorbed.

Reproduction

Guinea pigs are known for their ability to reproduce rapidly and prolifically. This is one of the reasons for their success as a food commodity in many South American cultures.

The female guinea pig can breed at the age of 4 weeks, but the healthiest young are born when she has reached at least 12 weeks of age. Males can breed when they are 8 to 9 weeks old.

Females go into heat every thirteen to twenty-one days. Babies are born anywhere from fifty-six to seventy-four days after birth. Litters usually range from one to thirteen babies, but four is most typical. The female guinea pig has only two teats with which to nurse her young, so many of the babies born in very large litters often do not survive.

The young are born with furry bodies and with their eyes open and can eat solid food within a day. They are weaned within three weeks to a month after birth, making them self-sufficient creatures at an early age.

FIND A VETERINARIAN

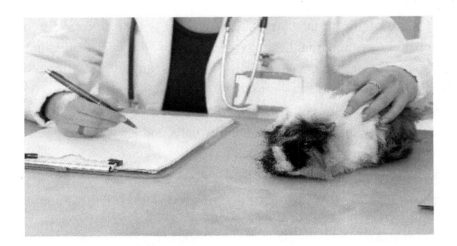

Many people think only cats and dogs need to go to a veterinarian. This is not true. Small mammals such as guinea pigs also deserve veterinary treatment if they become ill or injured.

Because your guinea pig's body varies greatly from that of a cat or dog, some of the treatments and drugs suitable for these other pets may be harmful to your guinea pig. Certain antibiotics commonly given to other small animals can kill a guinea pig. Given this, it's important only to use a vet who has experience in treating guinea pigs.

No matter what kind of pet you own, it's best not to wait until you have an emergency looking for a veterinarian. Since vets who specialize in treating guinea pigs are harder to find, selecting your guinea pig's veterinarian before she needs one is wise. The easiest way to locate a guinea pig vet is by referral. Ask other guinea pig owners who they use and whether they are happy with that individual or clinic.

Speak to the breeder or rescuer from whom you got your guinea pig. If you don't know any other guinea pig owners, you can also get the vet list from our official website guineapig101.com. They can help you locate a guinea pig veterinarian in your area. Or call your local county extension office and get the name and number of the guinea pig 4-H project leader in your area. They should be able to refer you to a veterinarian who treats guinea pigs.

Guinea pig in for an examination. The vet will be able to tell you if your pet has any potential health problems and will set up an appointment for a spay or neuter if you wish to have this surgery performed. This meeting will allow you to get to know the vet and give them the chance to start a file on your pet. It may also be a good time to ask your vet to teach you how to clip your guinea pigs nails and answer any questions about how to care for your new pet.

First Aid Kit

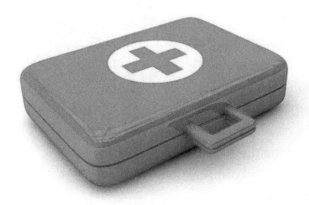

A first aid kit is often handy, whether it's for humans or animals. With the first aid kit, you can always treat some type of health condition, whether it's a simple or more complex one, before the vet or the doctor arrives.

When it comes to the first aid kit for a guinea pig, it's a great way to help your little furry pet. But, I feel obligated to mention that the first aid kit is something you can't rely on completely. When your guinea pig is sick, you can help it with your kit, but at the end of the day, you'll still need to visit the vet.

Before using the first aid kit, you need to educate yourself about Guinea pig health issues and diseases. This needs training, and because you're not a vet, you'll need the guidance of one.

You will learn a lot about common Guinea pig's health problems from the other articles on our website, but we'll focus on creating your guinea pig first kit aid.

Without any further ado, let's see how to start making one that has everything you are going to need. These first aid kits for pets come with only basics, and they require some extra components if you are going to use them for guinea pigs.

Here is a list of items you can include in the guinea pig first aid kit:

- Styptic powder
- Sterile saline flush solution
- Rubbing alcohol
- Betadine
- Chew Guard Spray
- Bacitracin antibiotic ointment
- Triple antibiotic ointment
- Styptic powder or Corn flour
- Acidophilus powder
- Eye ointment
- Eye drops
- Hydrogen peroxide
- Common antibiotics like Baytril, Bactrim, Metacam, Infacol, etc.
- Epson Salts
- vitamin c supplements or Probiotics powder
- Anti-fungal spray or ointment
- 1ml and 5ml syringe
- Clean towel
- Gauze pad
- Bandage
- First Aid Tape
- Cotton bud and Cotton balls
- Scissors
- Tweezers
- Heating pad and cold pack
- Small Animal Wipes

- Disposable gloves
- Weighing scale
- Guinea Pig Shampoo
- Coconut oil
- Oxbow critical care
- Oxbow Vitamin C supplements
- Small bowl and spoon

With all this in mind, you can now craft your guinea pig first aid kit. Make sure to contact your vet to see if you have the required ingredients and appropriate medications, in case you need it. The above list of first aid guinea pig kit contains all you need to treat the wounds and make your guinea pig healthy again.

OBSERVATION

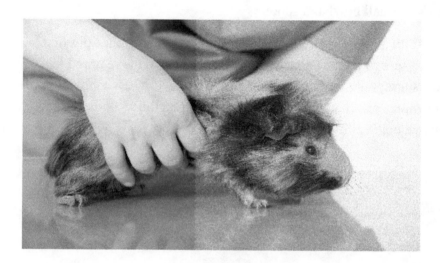

Get to know your guinea pig and keep a close eye on her. If you know how she looks when she is healthy, you'll be more likely to recognize signs of illness early on. Many illnesses that can be lethal are curable in their earliest stages. Realizing your guinea pig is under the weather before she becomes seriously ill could mean the difference between life and death.

Regular grooming is an important part of the observation since this hands-on procedure will encourage you to take a close look at your pet. The tasks required of regular grooming, such as maintaining your pet's nails and brushing, will prevent serious illness and injury.

Examine your guinea pigs cage floor or litter box regularly. Keep an eye out for diarrhea or lack of feces, all of which may indicate a problem.

PREVENTING DISEASE

If you follow the feeding and housing instructions in this book, your guinea pig should live a long and happy life. Furthermore, you should also take extra care to fend off infection and cope with issues effectively, should they come up.

DIET

Perhaps the single most important thing you will take to make sure your guinea pig remains healthy is to feed her a balanced diet. Your guinea pig has to eat those foods to ensure that her body systems function properly.

A correctly functioning system will help your guinea pig ward off some afflictions that often trouble less well-fed animals. When changing your guinea pig's diet or adding a portion of new food, remember always to do so gradually, slowly adding the new food in small amounts over time.

Sudden alteration of what your pet is eating will wreak havoc on her digestive system and cause her to become seriously ill.

An incredibly important item in your guinea pig's diet is water. Your guinea pig should always have access to clean, fresh water to keep her body functioning properly. Lack of water can result in some life-threatening conditions in guinea pigs.

Cleanliness

Another imperatively significant factor in keeping your guinea pig health is cleanliness. An unsanitary cage is a favorable place for ailment. Various illnesses can be directly traced to dirty floors, nest boxes, unclean food bowls, and water bottles. Consistently, remove fouled bedding material and fecal matter, and scrub your guinea pig's food dish and water bottle. Wash your pet's cage or hutch once every week to keep bacteria at the very least.

Stress

Like humans, guinea pigs are prone to stress. But contrary to most people, your guinea pig can't do much to change her life and alleviate the stress. She counts on you to do this for her. Stress has significant effects on the body's immune system. You may have noticed that you tend to catch colds more easily when you are under a great deal of stress.

The same applies to guinea pigs even though the illnesses they catch can be much more dangerous than the common cold. Do your best to minimize the stress on your guinea pig. This ensures that the animal should not be subject to loud noises, rough handling, extreme weather changes, or conditions that might scare her.

Guinea pigs require daily exercise and companionship as well and having this can minimize the amount of tension in the life of your pet. Keeping stress to a minimum will result in a guinea pig with a healthy immune system capable of fighting off the various bacteria, fungi, and parasites she may be exposed to.

Common Ailments

There are quite a few diseases that may affect a guinea pig, but others are rarely seen. What follows is a list of the most common pet guinea pig health problems today.

Abscesses

Abscesses are bacterial infections, which are the result of some kind of puncture wound. If your guinea pig slipped on something or had a battle with another pet, she may develop an abscess at the injury site. By its round appearance, you'll recognize an abscess, usually accompanied by a pus discharge. Your veterinarian will need antibiotic treatment for your guinea pig to help it fight off the infection.

Anal Impaction

Sometimes older, unneutered male guinea pigs suffer from a condition known as anal impaction. (Females and younger, neutered males may also develop this problem although it is uncommon.) This condition is caused by an anus muscle weakness, making it difficult for the cavy to pass fecal and cecal pellets.

Cavies with this problem have a hard lump around the rectal region, produce little to no feces, and start losing condition. When you think your guinea pig is having this problem, take him to a veterinarian.

Bladder Stones

Some guinea pigs are propended in their bladder to produce stones. Signs of this problem include squeaking and blood in the urine while urinating and defecating. The bladder stones can result in death if left untreated. If your guinea pig shows symptoms of this disease, seek urgent medical treatment.

Constipation/Diarrhea

Difficulty in defecating (constipation) or very loose stools (diarrhea) can be the result of poor diet or illness (a common cause of diarrhea is too many greens). Constipation symptoms weigh on defecation, lack of urine, distended belly, and lethargy. In general, diarrhea is detected by loose or runny stools and a dirty bottom. In this case, the doctor may need to decide what causes the problem and handle it.

Flies

Flies can be detrimental to guinea pigs in the open. We also lay their eggs on the soiled rectal region of a guinea pig, letting the larvae burrow into the skin and feeding on the flesh of the animal. Flies can be held at bay by making sure both the cage of your guinea pig and its fur are kept clean. If you have flies laying eggs on your guinea pig, call a veterinarian for help.

Heat Prostration

Guinea pigs are particularly susceptible to overheating. Do keep a close eye on your pet when the weather is hot. Heat prostration signs include stretched out posture, panting, quick breathing, and drooling. If you find your guinea pig in this state, move it out of the sun to a cool place and put a cold, wet towel around its body, or bathe it in cool water. Heat prostration is a state of emergency. Contact your veterinarian right away.

Lice

Lice are a problem specific to guinea pigs. These small, wingless insects live in infested guinea pigs' fur. Many pet guinea pigs are suffering from light lice infestations, which are not apparent to their owners. However, if the infestation gets heavy, the guinea pig will start scratching and losing fur and scabs can form on the skin.

When the guinea pig is suspected of having lice, take it to a doctor for treatment. Since guinea pig lice are easily spread to other guinea pigs (but not to humans), it is best to avoid associating your healthy pet with other members of her species that may be contaminated.

Malocclusion

If the front teeth of a guinea pig are not properly wearing down, the condition is known as malocclusion. This problem is usually the result of misaligned teeth, which are genetic.

Malocclusion signs include excessively long teeth, mouth infections, lip or tongue ulcerations, and difficulty eating. This is a common problem in guinea pigs and must be handled by a veterinarian, or eventually, the guinea pig will die. Treatment consists of a routine cutting or complete removal of the teeth.

Mites

Guinea pigs are vulnerable to a certain mite called Trixacarus cave. This mite causes the guinea pig to lose hair patches where the skin is turned red and scaly. Infested guinea pigs will play blindly and in circles.

Trixacarus mites are easily diffused from animal to animal. For assistance in the treatment of this parasite, contact your veterinarian.

Obesity

Veterinarians claim obesity in guinea pigs is a major health problem. Guinea pigs who are overweight are prone to some diseases that affect their major organs. In guinea pigs, the primary cause of obesity is overfeeding pellets and fruits.

Obese Guinea pigs should be put on a special diet to help them get down to their proper weight. If that does not result in a significant weight change in a month or so, check with your doctor for assistance.

Respiratory Infections

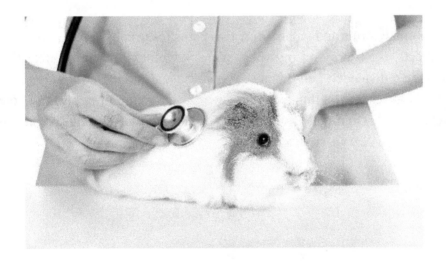

Guinea pigs are prone to some bacteria and viruses that can cause respiratory infections. Symptoms include sneezing, nose and eye discharge, loss of appetite, lethargy, and difficulty breathing. If a veterinarian is suspected of having a respiratory ailment, prompt treatment is necessary.

Scurvy

Because guinea pigs cannot produce their own vitamin C (like many other mammals), they are prone to scurvy, which is caused by a vitamin C deficiency.

A scurvy-stricken guinea pig may have a low appetite and swelled sore joints and arms. She'll be reluctant to move about and bleeding from the gums. This can be fatal if scurvy is untreated. A guinea pig with these signs should be taken right away to a doctor.

Sore Hocks

Guinea pigs that live in a wire-floor cage or hutch sometimes grow sore hocks. This condition is characterized by red, swollen skin on the hind legs, accompanied by a hair loss. The guinea pig can be hesitant to travel too. A veterinarian may provide the treatment with an antibiotic ointment along with a prescription for flooring improvement.

Worms

Roundworms and tapeworms, two parasites usually infected by dogs and cats, often prey on pigs of guinea. Symptoms of worm infestation include a distended belly, bad coat quality, and worms in or around the anus or feces. If you think you have worms on your guinea pig, call your veterinarian. Do not use an over-the-counter wormer for dogs or cats, as this might kill your guinea pig.

CHAPTER 9

COMMON PROBLEM OF A NEW GUINEA PIG OWNER

ALLERGIES TO GUINEA PIGS

No point contending exactly how adorable guinea pigs are. In any case, some people don't think of them as adorable, especially when they are hypersensitive to certain little rodents.

The most widely recognized indications of guinea-pig allergies are windedness, wheezing, runny nose, sniffling, and skin rashes, Be that as it may, the little, fluffy animal doesn't mean damage.

Regardless of whether you feel a portion of the signs while rewarding your pet or cleaning its cage, don't stress. Your best creature isn't at fault. The blood, discharges, or pee that has caused your allergies, not your scalp.

Step by step instructions to Deal with Guinea Pig Allergies

What's more, in the event of an unfavorably susceptible reaction, what do you do? Pet discoverer says seeing an allergist is the most significant activity by taking a check to survey the genuine wellspring of the allergies. You may think your cavy is causing your allergies; however, in all actuality, it was the roughage or other sheet material stuff.

Having built up that your pet is the wellspring of your allergies, here are five different ways to adapt to allergies to guinea pigs. These can assist with mitigating the throb, touchiness, and agony that you feel.

1. Antihistamines-This is utilized to battle unfavorably susceptible reactions quickly lighten the impacts of sensitivity. You will live with your response within a day or two. A few people determine encouragement by taking a hypersensitivity pill not long after they meet a guinea pig, and don't need to adapt to their petting's agonizing reactions. Your allergist should suggest a compelling antihistamine and will do as such.

2. Make use of decongestants – Many individuals who are adversely affected by guinea pigs discuss building up a swollen nose, or have respiratory issues. Utilizing a decongestant after rewarding your guinea pig will decrease your torment extensively if you are among them. You don't have to have a solution since decongestants are over-the-counter meds.

Likewise, you may have the decongestant nasal splash, which can be joined with an antihistamine for a more prominent advantage. Before buying the medication, it is anyway best to see a specialist. Have a remedy whether you experience difficulty with a pulse, swollen prostate, or a coronary condition.

3. Make use of a nasal corticosteroid treatment – A nasal splash is infused into the nose and scoured onto the nostril's external mass. It takes into account earnest nasal relief from discomfort. It doesn't require a solution, even though there are times when you need a remedy to get this prescription.

4. Make use of an air cleaner or purifiers- Getting some natural air is a quick way out of the house to maintain a strategic distance from allergens. Reestablishing the wellbeing back to typical will altogether limit respiratory side effects. An air channel or purifier additionally kills the hurtful allergens which mess skin up. Open the ventilation blinds, and get an air purifier when you start to encounter sensitivity side effects.

5. When you are asthmatic- whenever you handle a guinea pig, either utilize an inhaler or take asthmatic drugs on a remedy. Taking your asthma remedy facilitates your breathing issues without any problem.

Preventing Guinea Pig Allergies

There are things you can do to maintain a strategic distance from allergies to the guinea pigs. Next, put on two or three gloves; at that point, wear a veil before cleaning your pets cage. This adequately decreases the chance of getting into contact with the emissions of the creature. Since rewarding the guinea pig, strip and wash the pieces of clothing you had on. So, if it's commonsense, rather than doing it without anyone's help, you may ask another person to help you clean the cage.

Perhaps the most effortless method of preventing allergies isn't as a rule excessively near or, in any case contacting the guinea pig. So, what about not contacting your pet? Spot your pet on a cover or towel to limit the chance of building up hypersensitivity. At the point when you're set, you'll have to ensure you wash the towel a short time later. Other than that, after every single involvement in your guinea pig, you must wash your hands.

Ought not to lie on your pad, love seat, or another spot to unwind with your feline. Spot your cavy's enclosure in another room beyond what many would consider possible, not your room.

Bottom line

Attempt a portion of the treatment choices when the allergies are caused, yet when the sickness declines, it is ideal to attempt an expert. Review continually making the preparatory strides talked about to hold allergies under control.

Smells bad

Guinea pigs make extraordinary pooches. Many of you have or have kept cavies at home in the past expertise much bliss they bring to your family unit. Holding your prosperity can be a troublesome undertaking, be that as it may. Guinea pigs are powerless against certain basic ailments and infections.

Common Health Issues in Guinea Pigs

1. Abscesses
2. Scurvy
3. Diarrhea
4. Respiratory tract infections
5. Infections due to lice, mites, or fungus

In this segment, you'll read about the most popular problems guinea pigs continue to suffer from and how you, the owner of the pet, should be able to deal with these issues.

1. Respiratory Tract Infections

Infections of the respiratory tract or URIs are a lethal bacterial disease that can prompt the passing of your guinea pig whenever left unchecked. Most pet shops are ceaselessly dealing with guinea pigs, which were delivered with URIs to their shop. That is why it's more secure to bring a guinea pig up in many circumstances instead of buying one from a pet shop. Signs if the guinea pig has a URI, include:

- Lethargy
- A rough-looking or puffed up coat
- Crusty eyes or eyes that are almost sealed shut
- Sneezing/Coughing
- Delayed breathing or wheezing
- No feces (as a result of not eating)
- Refusal to eat or drink

On the off chance that you see any of these indications, you will rapidly take your guinea pig to an outlandish vet! At that point, the vet will manage the standard registration to guarantee the guinea pig has a URI. They will test for hydration, test their lungs and heart, and take x-ray to perceive how much water they have. They will, at that point, as a rule, run a piggy verify which anti-infection agents are better fit for them.

2. Diarrhea

When you think your guinea pig has diarrhea, please see a doctor immediately. It is a strong sign of a very severe bowel condition if you find a black watery sort of stool in the cage, followed by a foul-smelling odor. Mild cases of diarrhea are caused by over-feeding the guinea pig with fruits and vegetables. When the discharge is serious enough for a doctor to look at your piggy, there are a couple of things they'll do:

- Fecal float: This procedure is used to detect bacteria in the feces of the guinea pig.
- Gram Stains: Each test shows the approximate amount of gram-negative and gram-positive bacteria present on the guinea pig's feces.
- Culture: This test shows the bacteria in your guinea pig can cause discomfort.

When there is an immediate danger to your guinea pig's life, the doctor will talk you through a few measures to get your piggyback nursed back to safety. Whether antibiotics are required, your doctor will then prescribe your piggy needs the right medications.

3. Scurvy

Like humans, guinea pigs cannot produce their own vitamin C. We have to give them the right amount of vitamin C each day, so they don't get scurvy. Signs if the guinea pig does have scurvy include:

- Internal skeletal-muscular hemorrhage
- Tenderness to touch (will not let you touch, pick up, or hold them)
- Eye and nose discharge
- Weight loss
- Unwillingness to move, lethargy, or weakness
- Hopping instead of walking or trotting

Many pet shops sell vitamin C pills that can be consumed by your guinea pig or dumped into their water bottles. Many of the time, guinea pigs do not take the tablets and refuse to drink their water if they place the droplets in their cups of water. So, to be safe, do NOT add the vitamin C drops to your guinea pigs drink. Speak to your veterinarian about which fruits, vegetables, and pellet diets giving your piggy the best amount of Vitamin C.

4. Abscesses

Abscesses are caused by so many things and are not common in guinea pigs. Abscesses are caused by:

- Internal problems
- Unclean cage and environment
- A bite or scratch wound inflicted by another guinea pig or pet
- Malnutrition

When you spot a lump or bulge growing on your guinea pig's body, it is safe to take it to the vet quickly. Possibly a few things might be off, and it could not even be an abscess! It could be just a few things like

- Trichofolliculoma
- Thyroid adenoma
- Mammary tumor

- Lipoma
- Cyst
- Cervical Lymphadenitis

A few checks are mandatory to figure out which illness the piggy has. In most cases, whether there is an abscess or other skin mass caused by another condition, they would have to lance and remove the lump most often as long as it is not a tumor and as long as it is not cancer. Your vet will be sending you two other drugs following the operation, an infectious treatment, and a pain reliever.

5. Skin Parasites

Guinea pigs generally brush themselves, but if you see your guinea pig constantly itching and sometimes losing hair, your piggy may be serious. In guinea pigs, the most common parasite is mange mite.

This causes appalling agony to guinea pigs and needs care with ASAP! Many parasites are common in guinea pigs, known as cavy lice, which chirodiscoids (which is a harmless fur mite but still should be treated).

The famous flea and tick medicine veterans said Advantage works on lice, but it does not treat mange mites. Avoid using any shampoos on the guinea pigs, flea, or mouse. The vet should be sure to supply you with a specific prescription for the skin and hair that can be added to your guinea pig and any shampoos that might be appropriate.

YOU AND YOUR PET

Your guinea pig must have regular checkups. Consider them dogs and cats, and why not guinea pigs? Choose an exotic vet near you, and take your piggy for a routine check-in every few months. If you ever find obvious signs of distress or odd behavior, make sure to take your piggy to the vet. Your guinea pig might be a major concern, and you might not even know it!

Please bear in mind that Guinea pigs are prey animals. Hence, they do not show any symptoms of illness in most cases until it is too late for treatment. Just keep an eye on the guinea pig, and these are habits. Just make sure they sleep and search their water bottle regularly to see what they've been eating. Lower level of bottled water mean they have been drinking much water.

TRAVELING AND LEAVING MY GUINEA PIG BEHIND

Holidays are what we all like now and then. It's time we enjoy ourselves without the workload, busy lives, and animals? Small animals are much more difficult to bear. No one needs to carry around their cage, their veggies, their water bottle, and their hay.

Veterinarians sell your dogs and cats room and board, but what about your little guinea pig's housing?

How to keep your guinea pig's healthy and safe when you leave your guinea pig alone Whether you're going on a weekend or a trip and you're planning to leave your guinea pigs alone, you need to take some care.

You can't just chuck any leftover food away and leave them alone. Like we'd shared before, the guinea pigs will get into all kinds of trouble before they're home.

Therefore, we need to make sure our piggies remain well and safe while we're gone. It is vital not only for them but also for you because you can relax and fly with peace of mind that even though you are not around, they will be okay.

Get a pet sitter

When you're going to keep your guinea pigs alone for more than a day, you'll need to consider getting someone to look after them for a nominal fee.

Today, depending on where you live and what services you have at your fingertips, there will be many choices. You can either hire a daily pet sitter to see your guinea pigs once in a while or leave your guinea pig back in their place or center to look after your piggies.

When these facilities are not available, you should also ask Kennels in the city who will be happy to look after the guinea pigs likewise. For a pair of guinea pigs, you can expect to pay a nominal fee of 5-10 $a day. If you're planning to leave them for a long time or have a big litter size, you could bargain slightly.

Train a friend or a neighbor to take care of your guinea pigs

If a pet sitter or kennel is not a choice for you, finding a neighbor or a relative to look after your guinea pigs will be the second-best solution.

When you're going for a day then you would have no trouble leaving them alone; but, if you're planning to go for more than a day than it will be a smart idea to pack all the vegetables and place them in a refrigerator jar and get loads of hay in tiny sacks.

Walking in and tossing food in the cage, and refilling their water bottles, would be easy for your friend and neighbor. If you intend to leave for a weekend or more, this is one of the most effective methods.

Set up a camera to monitor them from your phone

When you are a frequent traveler who frequently has to leave your guinea pigs behind for a day or two, you may need to consider installing a surveillance camera with links to live phone videos.

This way, you can closely track your guinea pigs in short periods to make sure they do well. When you encounter issues of any kind, you might ask your friends, relatives, or neighbor to find them out.

How long can you leave a guinea pig unattended?

It is rarely recommended that cavies be left unattended for longer than 24 hours, but they can be left alone for 48 hours without drastic results.

Never leave your guinea pig home for longer than this, because there is so much time to go wrong with things. Even it is pressing for 48 hours, as cavies need good treatment and attention. Give them extra food if you're going to leave them for a day, add an extra water bottle, and throw in extra hay. It is also strongly advised to disinfect the cage as a stinky cage is very uncomfortable coming home. Without proper planning sending, someone alone is a big no-no.

Occasions can happen where you may need to travel, so you will still have a list of people you can trust to take care of your guinea pig. Part of having a pet is taking care of them or making sure they're cared for properly. Their satisfaction is up to you.

Guinea Pig Cage cleaning

C&C cages are meant to be clean on the spot. There's no need to raise the foundation from the edge of the grid and remove it and spray it down outside. This is needless and unworkable.

Sprinkle the interior of the coroplast foundation with a combination of half water / half white vinegar after cleaning the bedding, then scrub clean with a cloth, paper towels, or a gentle brush. Rinse and cover the bedding with a cool, moist towel. When you clean the cages, your guinea pigs will be happier and healthier! They are looking up to you to make that happen.

Basics of Cleaning the Cage

Daily

How to clean your cage daily or as needed.

- Remove any food and discard the obscene amount.
- Clear any stacks of loose hay and substitute it with fresh hay (if outside of a hayrack).
- Using a rigid brush and mini powder pan or mini vacuum to clean up any leftover fleece poos
- Remove any dirty, soiled pieces in the kitchen area — mix them or add fresh, dry bedding.
- If appropriate, remove any Fleece pads.
- Load the hay rack up — leave it still loaded to capacity.
- Hold the freshwater in Bottle

Weekly.

Cleaning of a complete cage at least weekly or as needed.

- Clean the Coroplast with half water / half white vinegar spray bottle.
- Wash the kitchen area or litter tub, drain it and thoroughly clean it with the vinegar solution.
- Remove all the bedding with fleece. Once you cut the fleece lining, pick the poos either in the cage or shake/brush them off,

depending on what works for you. Put a hard brush off the fleece to scrape dirt, hay, and poos. Many people consider a lint roller on their hair effective for them.

- Spray the fleece cleanly with transparent detergent. Apply half of the vinegar to a full cup to reduce odor and help disinfect. Cold to rain. NO dryer cushions or texture conditioners. The objective is to make fleece as porous as could be expected under the circumstances; synthetic concoctions stop up the pores.
- Please remove the lint trap from your dryer after each wash.
- In the Kitchen area, replace with whatever fresh bedding you are using.
- Spray water bottles well with a bottle cleaner, including their snouts.
- Swap a rack of hay with new hay.
- Clean any cozies as appropriate and ensure that all potty pads inside are clean and safe.

How often should you clean your cage?

Spot Cleanings vs. Full Cleanings

Timing is a problem considering our unusual seven-day weeks. For arranging the need for refreshments cannot fit well. You almost always want to do at least once a week a complete cage wash, usually on the weekend, because you have more time and energy to commit to being thorough. That makes the cage refresh more of a challenge every 2, 3, or 4 days. You are going to have to figure this out. You'll need to work that out. Under the best of bedding circumstances, you'll need to refresh midweek and full clean once a week. Sometimes, you need to refresh or clean every other day. Sometimes every 3 days. Some people clean it every single day. Everyone is different. But, "once a week" attention is NOT good enough. Dirty cages can be a life-threatening health hazard to your guinea pig.

The main point is how often the cage is clean. Guinea pigs should never lie in damp bedding or fleece damp. You wouldn't want your baby to wander around too long in a muddy, messy diaper. The same is true of our treatment for caged animals.

It is not only smelly and gross for them, but it is also dangerous. It's there in their hands. The piling up of ammonia is a much worse environmental threat than any pine shaving phenols (smell) ever would be. URIs (upper respiratory infections) and difficult-to-treat blunder feet are perilous sicknesses that can be welcomed on by filthy confines.

They are also favorite places for infection invasions, microscopic organisms, molds, and parasitic infections, such as ringworm. Keeping your cage secure is necessary. Perfect? Each day spot clear.

Cleaning the Cage Details

Vinegar is a perfect remedy for cleaning.

- A spray bottle is repurposed and filled with half water, half white vinegar. It works well to vacuum out the cage's Coroplast floors and walls.
  Not only is vinegar by the gallon anti-microbial, anti-bacterial, anti-fungal, and super inexpensive, it's an acid. Urine is the reason for this. Acids neutralize bases. Vinegar does a fine job of removing and purifying urine. And of course, it is food and guinea pig safe, need to waste money on more bottles of plastic and other chemicals polluting the environment.
- 1/2 to 1 cup of white vinegar add to the bedding wash
  In addition to the fact that vinegar works incredible on the Coroplast, it encourages by applying it to your wool washer to disinfect and freshen up you're down. Heavily soiled materials may be washed in vinegar to help get them back to life. Vinegar helps to keep the fleece moist and to wick well.

Truly tough acrylic stains?

Soak it up with a few hours with flat vinegar. Wash, scrub, and rinse off; repeat as needed. The Coroplast must come up. Note to yourself, though — you're not doing the bedding right if you have super tough marks on your fabric. You would need to change the bedding framework, vacuum it all the more regularly, or join the two.

In general, poor stains are a warning that the guinea pigs are not getting proper caging treatment.

Cleaning off a Midwest Cage Canvas?

Not that fast. For this reason, we suggest replacing the Midwest cage canvas bottom with a walled, Coroplast insert. Or on the other hand, utilizing a Fleece Flippers as a sheet material that incorporates a Coroplast fix to help keep water from slipping into the texture spread.

The more you brush and clean the paint, the more the 'water-safe' surface is focused on, leaving it significantly more powerless to rust, wreckage, and jetsam and soil amassing. Even though our Coroplast embed tackles the cleaning issue, all other levels, plastic-upheld or water-safe confine liners, don't shield the canvas dividers from direct pee hits or pee gushing from the corners and dividers underneath. You simply need to do whatever you can.

CHAPTER 10

GUINEA PIG PREGNANCY

FALSE PREGNANCY (PHANTOM PREGNANCY)

Phantom pregnancy is a disease when someone displays the pregnancy signs, but ultimately, they are not pregnant. This is a growing issue in dogs and rabbits, but what about our guinea pigs?

Could guinea pigs have a phantom or false pregnancy?

Indeed, a guinea pig may have a phantom conception, right after being spayed. Yet there is nothing important to think about this because they will know in about three weeks that they are not pregnant, and then they will return to life.

At this point, your guinea pig will need empathy and help from you. At this time, her hormones would be highly erratic. This is also likely that you have to treat mood swings, increased appetite, and odd habits.

What is the phantom of false pregnancy in guinea pigs?

False paternity is also known as false pregnancies or pseudo pregnancy; it occurs when a guinea pig is told that she is pregnant, but she is not. It is normal in any female guinea pig of breeding age.

Compared to a guinea pig, there is little distinction between phantom and true conception. She will act like she is pregnant, but she is not.

What causes phantom pregnancies in guinea pigs?

It's a fantasy that is shaped by the guinea pig and lasts for about 20 days. Now and again, it may last somewhat more or shorter.

At the point when female guinea pigs ovulate, she accepts that she is pregnant, although she isn't. Overemphasize can also be a reason for phantom pregnancies. Let us understand this very well.

1. Overstressed: If a guinea pig gets focused on, they may ovulate, and then they create confusion that they are pregnant. There are many ways the guinea pig can be nervous. For example: - Loud sounds, Fear of gatecrasher, and so on.

2. Separated from a bonded friend: Guinea pigs can get discouraged whenever separated from their bonded partner because they are exceptionally used to their quality. The abrupt disappearance of their partner will make them fall under pain.

3. Taken to the vet: Guinea pigs despise medication and health tests. An outing to the vet can cause worry in your guinea pigs.

How long does a phantom pregnancy last?

Guinea pig's phantom pregnancy can last up to 20-30 days, and it can last longer now and again. Pregnancy isn't that pleasant for guinea pigs. According to research, approx 20 percent of pregnant guinea pigs pass away during conception.

However, the stronger ones among them endure with a ton of issues, which brings about costly to you and unpleasant to her.

Guinea pig's pregnancy lasts from 9 to 10 weeks. Guinea pig's false pregnancy can last up to 20-30 days, and it can last longer at times. The timetable of fake conception versus real conception plays out as follows:

DAY 1

Genuine Pregnancy

The un-spayed guinea pigs mates with an unneutered male and is impregnated.

Fake Pregnancy

In this case, the guinea pigs ovulate due to stress and consider that she is pregnant.

DAY 7-12

Genuine Pregnancy

She will start eating more and more as she is eating for 4-5 babies.

Fake Pregnancy

In this case, she will eat more and become aggressive towards other guinea pigs.

DAY 15-18

Genuine Pregnancy

The tummy starts getting swollen and might have small bumps.

Fake Pregnancy

No change in guinea pigs tummy

DAY 20-25

Genuine Pregnancy

A Guinea pig will start making the nest. The guinea pig will stockpile hay and blankets.

Fake Pregnancy

A Guinea pig will start making the nest. The guinea pig will stockpile hay and blankets.

DAY 30-38

Genuine Pregnancy

The nesting process begins; the guinea pigs start resting and relaxing in her nest.

Fake Pregnancy

The guinea pig will start losing interest in nesting and will come back to its normal behavior.

DAY 50-60

Genuine Pregnancy

The guinea pig will give birth.

Fake Pregnancy

Your guinea pig till now has forgotten everything related to her phantom pregnancy.

Guinea pig phantom pregnancies treatment

We will propose you make your guinea pig comfortable when she is encountering a false pregnancy. You can make her comfortable by offering them food and some part of hay. They will eat some hay, and others will be used for making a home. Do whatever it takes not to upset your guinea pig as that time she will be irritable and territorial.

This may be likely that your guinea pig isn't pleased with you washing their tank. In any case, you, despite everything, have to do it to maintain appropriate cleanliness, as the unclean condition can lead to significant issues to your guinea pig.

How Do I Know If My Guinea Pig Is Pregnant?

The moment you realize that your guinea pig is pregnant, you should be planning to take it to the vet because there might be many risks coming, most especially if your pet is older than a year old and has never had a litter before. Here are two or three principle structures wherein you can say that your guinea pig is envisioning.

So, the most legitimate approach is to pick if your pet has been in contact with an unneutered male beginning late? Guinea pigs accomplish sexual maturity prior, notwithstanding when they are just five to about a month and a half old. Any gatekeepers have taken a female guinea pig home because to find that she is starting at now pregnant!

If your guinea pig has been pregnant for more than half a month, you may have the option to feel the fetuses in your pet extremely tenderly. Without turning her over or applying some pressure on her, place your hands carefully over her sides to feel the babies in her tummy.

When you keep her firmly by the arms while she's on your lap or a towel, you will have the option to delicately feel the bumps and knocks as you slip your left hand around her delicately. Bunches may mean piglets; however, they can likewise mean medical problems. For instance, blisters say it's a brilliant idea to take them to the vets for a test or advise on how the pregnancy is progressing and their well-being.

Watch out for what your guinea pig eats. Since pregnant sows are making other guinea pigs inside them, they'll need to eat unmistakably more than anticipated, now and again a couple of times their typical sum. In any case, in case your other guinea pigs are eating more too, then this could be characteristic of the cold rather than pregnancy.

At long last, on the off chance that your guinea pig has full-grown-up, you can screen her weight to attempt to distinguish whether or not she is pregnant. You actually won't have the option to do that without a suitable instrument, since she's just going to add on a couple of grams a day.

If you gauge her each week, you should have the option to see noticeable contrasts on the off chance that she is pregnant. Toward the finish of the birth, her litter should be more than twice her body weight, and she will be about twofold the sum she normally conceived.

In case you discover any of these effects, and then I will give you a head up to take your guinea pig to the vet. That way, if one of these signs isn't because of pregnancy, you can get your guinea pig the correct treatment, because on the off chance that your pet ends up being pregnant, then the vet will make sure that there are no complications, as well as offer you some guidance regarding how best to care for the guinea pig previously and during her introduction to the world.

Pregnancy symptoms:

How about we investigate normal real pregnancy symptoms:

Ballooning abdomen: As each female delivers a baby, their abdomen gets the chance to develop. It is with the female guinea pigs; when they become pregnant, they get a swollen uterus.

Eating more: It is regular to eat more at the hour of birth because there are 4-5 bars inside guinea pigs' stomachs. The appetite level of your guinea pigs additionally raises since they need more food as they are thinking about 4-5 youngsters.

Mood Fluctuations: Only the best guinea pig can get flightier. Pregnancy prompts significant mood swings, which are the clarification for dissatisfaction in guinea pigs.

Nesting: Whenever a guinea pig is pregnant, she will set up a home. At whatever point you see your guinea pig conveying roughage in her mouth for making a home, you can think about it as a symptom of pregnancy.

It will be hard to choose whether she is pregnant or not, as she will have indistinguishable activities from ordinary pregnancy.

She will participate in this conduct for at any rate 20-30 days, and after this, a ghost pregnancy goes to a sudden end, and guinea pigs come back to typical. There is a substitute method to check whether your guinea pig is pregnant or not.

You can move your finger around her midsection and keeping in mind that doing that, on the off chance that you feel little bumps, at that point, consider your guinea pig as pregnant.

On the off chance that you don't feel anything while moving fingers around her tummy, she isn't pregnant at that point.

What is the length of a guinea pig pregnancy?

The guinea pig pregnancy period is long – between 59-72 days (the normal is 65 days) the length of a guinea pig pregnancy depends on the litter size (for example, the smaller the litter, the longer the period of the guinea pig pregnancy).

The actual timeframe of pregnancy for one litter of guinea pig is about 70 days; for a litter of 6 guinea pigs, it is about 67 days. First liters are always smaller than later litters. Females can get huge during birth.

Deciding the number of babies is essential. It is additionally important to assess the number of babies in the belly with the goal that you can be certain the mother has brought forth all the babies and isn't having issues delivering them all (assists with ensuring no babies left in the belly).

What are the foods pregnant guinea pigs should eat?

You should take care of your pregnant guinea pigs by giving them a food routine consisting of:

- A little of top-notch commercial pellet
- A Lot of Vitamin C rich nourishments, for example, kiwi organic product or citrus
- Green leafy vegetables
- Grass as well as grass feed
- A limited quantity of Alfalfa hay – Although this is not so significant (as a food supplement to give expanded calcium and protein to your guinea pigs).

How easy is the guinea pigs' birth?

Having an unpleasant pregnancy is very common among guinea pigs, so it's good to see your vet for further advice about the thought of pregnant guinea pigs and the birthing method. While some guinea pigs can conceive an offspring normally and unassisted, others need veterinary assistance to conceive an offspring (some may require prescriptions or potentially a cesarean area).

You should decide with your vet when your guinea pig is probably going to conceive an offspring and to watch her near guarantee she gets veterinary assistance ought to there be any issues.

Pregnancy ketosis

This is possibly a hard moment that usually occurs in some pregnant guinea pigs during late pregnancy or inside a couple of long periods of pregnancy. The predisposing factors incorporate weight (>800 grams), fasting (not being taken care of sufficiently), on the off chance that it is the first or second pregnancy, change in diet, stress, and heredity.

The indications of pregnancy blood poisoning are the unexpected beginning of melancholy (peaceful, feeble, and dormant) and anorexia (not eating). They may likewise experience issues breathing and show muscle constrictions. Risk decrease incorporates forestalling corpulence in the mother guinea pig and giving satisfactory vitality in the eating routine late in incubation.

A few specialists suggest including a limited quantity of glucose to the mother's savoring water late pregnancy as a preventive measure (if you don't mind counsel your vet about this first).

AFTER THE BIRTH

Newborn guinea pigs will start eating much food during the initial barely any days' post-birth. Weaning is a continuous showing process which happens over some undefined time frame (around half a month). Infant guinea pigs must be kept with their mother until the weaning method has finished, the infant guinea pigs can deal with unreservedly, and they are at any rate a month mature enough.

Infants' guinea pigs are sexed by investigating the external genitalia (your vet can assist in sexing the children). Arriving at the sexual maturity stage is very common in guinea pigs.

Females can arrive at sexual maturity as right on time as around four a month and a half old enough and males as ahead of schedule as roughly 8-9 weeks old enough so the diverse genders ought to be isolated before they can imitate with one another. Note that infant guinea pigs must be with their mother until the weaning procedure is finished, and they can freely take care of them.

Guinea pigs can fall pregnant again straight after bringing forth their litter – so whole grown-up male guinea pigs must be kept independently from females in late pregnancy and after the birth to forestall any further undesirable/spontaneous litters of child guinea pigs.

BABY GUINEA PIGS

omestic guinea pigs originated in South America, but these articulate, friendly animals live in homes all over the world today. Guinea pigs are kept as family pets and bred for a show like dogs, cats, and rabbits.

The American Cavy Breeders Association, which regulates breed standards and events in the United States, formalizes the New Guinea pig breeds. Whether you're hoping to rear your litter of Abyssinian guinea pigs, or you're hoping to purchase a Peruvian baby guinea pig, it's important to be able to understand how they grow and mature naturally for the species and their breed.

What Are Baby Guinea Pigs Called?

Little guinea pigs are known as pups. The term pup calls to mind baby dogs, but guinea pigs currently belong to a rat animal family called cavies. The male guinea pigs are called boars as they grow up, and the females are called sows. Much like huge pigs in the farmyard!

There's no set time when a guinea pig becomes an adult and ceases being a child. Yet most people believe that when they reach sexual maturity, they are only four weeks old. You could hear them identified as 'juniors' between then and hitting their maximum adult weight several months later.

How many babies do guinea pigs have?

There are several small animals (think rats and rabbits) that have a reputation as successful breeders. And guinea pigs are likewise very prolific little animals! Guinea pig litters can have up to eight pups, but more common are two, three, or four.

The Guinness Book of World Records registered the largest guinea pig litter containing a whopping 17 pups!

How Often Do Guinea Pigs Have Babies?

Although they will breed year-round, springtime is the prime window for baby guineas to emerge.

Guinea pig sows can become pregnant again within hours of conception.

Because their gestation only takes 59-73 days, in principle, a female guinea pig is capable of carrying five or even six liters a year.

This would put tremendous pressure on her body and her intellectual stamina, though.

Therefore, caring for breeders isn't good enough.

What does a baby Guinea Pig look like?

Newborn guinea pigs weigh 60 g-115 g. An average size pup weighs about 3 to 5 inches at birth and is very cylindrical - in fact, about the size of a tangerine!

Person size is usually related to litter size, and the younger they are each likely to be, the more siblings there are in a group.

Their paws and heads compared to their bodies are comically outsized, and they even have a full coat of hair. Their tiny mouths already excel in producing 20 teeth, which are constantly increasing.

Baby Guinea Pigs Week by Week

Guinea pig pregnancy appears to be brief, but its duration still lasts a surprisingly long period. And the result is guinea pig babies are now being born more mature than many other species. It is termed 'precociousness.' for example, guinea pigs are born with their eyes open, and so they can feel their ears – which appear enormous at the moment. So, the remaining milestones left to watch have to do with development, eating, behavior, and sexual maturity.

Young Guinea pigs – Week One

Guinea pig babies are born very fast. Upon delivery, all the pups normally arrive within half an hour. They would start wriggling and running around as soon as their mom licked them clean.

And nursing should be defined within a few hours. Yet another noteworthy thing about baby guinea pigs is how big their appetite is!

What Do Baby Guinea Pigs Eat?

Baby guinea pigs can eat solid food very rapidly (within hours) after birth. They will start eating turf, fruit, hay, and pellet feed much like adults within twenty-four hours.

Witnessing may be a bit shocking, but it's natural, and there's nothing to think about. Despite being able to feed almost instantly, baby guineas still need to nurse and will try milk about every two hours.

Can You Touch a Newborn Guinea Pig?

It's good to gently treat your new guinea pig pups during their first week, but make sure always give them plenty of time with their mum. Too early treating them will break the relationship they need with their mom to feed on her and huddle for comfort against her. This can, at worst, drive her to deny them.

When handling a newborn guinea pig, beware of going slowly and softly. Face-to-face approach to them, and they can see you coming. Place one hand beneath their tummy, and one hand behind their back, and hold it close to you.

Two-Week-Old Baby Guinea Pigs

In their second week, you can't ignore how much your baby guinea pigs have already grown. You may be struck by how busy and outgoing they are.

During this time, you might expect your baby Guinea pigs to wonder eagerly around their environment, but their legs are still a little shaky, and unexpectedly they are likely to plop down while they discover their surroundings. Guinea pigs are also well-known communicators, and from babyhood, they continue vocalizing.

What Do Baby Guinea Pigs Sound Like?

Guinea pigs make 11 different forms of calls. They use them to form social connections and facilitate bonding, draw herd members' attention over long distances, express distress, and sound the alarm. And baby guinea pigs will join in from a very young age. Don't be surprised if your pup lets out a little chirp as a way to order milk!

You may also note that when you drive them away from their mother, they squeak in fear. If that happens, drop them back in with her, and then visit again. Paying plenty of short visits with your mother to your litter and getting them used to soft care without thinking about them would be a critical basis for successful socialization.

Socializing Baby Guinea Pigs

A significant part of rearing happy, comfortable pets is having guinea pigs accustomed to handling from an early age. It's just as necessary to share the rest of your baby guinea pig with other guinea pigs. That is where they learn how to act and interact inside a group.

For the first two weeks, it is easy to do by holding the whole litter together with their parents, but next week it is time to start worrying about splitting them.

Three-Week-Old Baby Guinea Pigs

Three weeks mark the first stage that pups can deter their mother from breastfeeding, yet other vets are suggesting weaning the pups as late as six weeks.

Weaning age is based on many factors, including the pup's weight, the supply of milk to the mother, and the number of siblings. Yet normally, at about the 3rd week, mom will start stopping her babies from breastfeeding. It is the age, substantially, when pups tend to reach sexual maturity.

So, this means that it is time for the boys to move to a new home in a mixed litter of boys and girls to avoid unnecessary pregnancies.

How Do You Sex Baby Guinea Pigs?

No matter how adorable baby guinea pigs are, there would be enough for most people to care about one litter at a time. Allowing siblings to mate often provides their children with the possibility of serious congenital abnormalities. Sexing baby mice is notoriously difficult, and the best way to be sure which of your pups are girls and which are boys is to ask for guidance from a more seasoned trainer or a vet.

Start by softly holding onto their back, your guinea pig. Be prepared to quickly judge them, as they do not enjoy being left in that role for long! Male baby guinea pigs face their anus with a donut-shaped genital gap. When you run a finger closely over the area, you should feel their penis shaft under the surface. So, if you press very softly, it might be that the penis emerges.

By comparison, female baby guinea pigs have a y-shaped genital gap positioned far closer to the anus. And of course, you do not feel a penis when you run a finger over the region!

Baby Guinea Pig Behavior – Week Four Onwards

By the time they're a month old, the body form of baby guinea pigs resembles quite that of a hamster from Syria. You're going to get a kick out of their eagerness to catch each other and play around, and maybe even start popcorning.

Popcorning is an extremely succinct term to describe the rapid leaping, to bump and hopping movements of frenzied guinea pigs. Individuals are going to continue showing their own distinct identities too. So, all the habits they'll need to do on their own instead of being done by a mom for them – like grooming – would be well known. At this point, you might have noticed them beginning to join in with social grooming.

How Long Do Baby Guinea Pigs Stay with Their Mothers?

Around six weeks old infant guinea pigs are fully weaned, and their mother has finished breastfeeding. They've learned all the freedom skills they need, and they're excited to leave the nest.

The age at which most breeders will have their pups go to their new homes is six to seven weeks old. That is also the age of baby guinea pig's smallest in pet shops.

How to Care for Baby Guinea Pigs

If you are taking your baby guinea pig back home at the age of seven weeks, you will find all the details you need to raise in our guide to guinea pigs as pets. Keep an eye on their weight, and you'll be able to watch them accumulate ounces slowly until after their first birthday.

If you think a baby guinea pig is too small or fails to succeed, please visit your vet. Bathing them will wait until they are at least eight weeks old if it's something you want to do.

Baby Guinea Pig Care – Raising a Litter of Pups

On the other hand, if you're going to help a sow grow from birth a litter of pups, there's something to worry about.

- Give your litter the perfect start before your sow is even born – make sure she gets a clean bill of health from a doctor until it is matted, then buy a hutch big enough to hold her than her babies before they move out.
- During birth, your sow will require plenty of calories and vitamin C, so make sure that your hay doesn't run out and give fresh fruit and vegetables more support.
- Turn her bedding up to labor every day even when the pups are small. Ammonia emissions from soiled bedding can damage the pups' lungs, and when she is breastfeeding, bacteria can invade the nipples of your sows.
- Before the pups arrive, track them closely and ensure that breastfeeding is completed within 12 hours. Contact the vet for advice should that be the case.
- Continue providing shredded lettuce to them from the day of their birth. Remember to remove any that leave, as it will spoil quickly.

- The pups must know a lot – from the parents, they stay with, how to establish social ties and which food is healthy and consume. Think about how you can ensure the boys will get this education after abandoning their mother and siblings at the age of three weeks.

Do Guinea Pigs Eat Their Babies?

Unfortunately, enough, mothers of guinea pigs often eat their young newborns. It can be disconcerting and disturbing. Feeling this is understandable. Yet it's better to stop understanding the biological causes that it happens.

This can happen on two ways.

1. Unfamiliarity.

An inexperienced sow could inadvertently damage her teeth when attempting to clean them up after birth. It generally occurs when pups are stillborn to survive, or born to sick.

She continues to scrub them more aggressively when they don't respond to her touch before finally, she destroys them.

2. Unnourished

Second, if she's seriously malnourished, even an accomplished guinea pig mom might revert to eating her kids. Holding that in mind doesn't automatically mean she's incredibly thin.

When there are not enough essential vitamins and minerals in her diet, she will also be malnourished while consuming enough calories to keep her body weight going.

CONCLUSION

Before you get a guinea pig, know that you are taking on a long-term investment, as these little furry squeakers will keep you from five to seven years of the company for anywhere. Providing proper housing, food, toys, grooming, daily interaction, and periodic vet visits to your pet during this time are essential to his well-being. Proteins in the Piggy's urine and saliva are the culprits when it comes to allergies.

Minimizing shedding can give some relief, as hair often helps transmit allergens when you're dealing with your pet. Guinea pigs make amazing pets for so many people. They are small and cute, and the majority of guinea piggies love to be held at stroked for ages.

In the wild guinea pigs or cavies, they are also known as living in herds and are social animals. This means that the majority of pigs, especially the sows (females) are very friendly. Of course, when you first get one, you are likely to be shy, but after your new pet gets to know you, he or she is likely to be very friendly.

Compared with other pets, guinea pigs don't take up as much time - after all, you don't need to walk your piggie every day, although they will still need regular exercise. You'll need to carry out a basic care routine every day, which includes: feeding, giving water, grooming, checking health, giving your piggie exercise, and at least once a week was cleaning out a hutch or cage.

Cavies are creatures of routine, so you should allocate a time each day, at the same time, for feeding, e.t.c.

Many people find that guinea piggies make excellent first pets for children as they help to teach them about responsibility for animals. Of course, a pet shouldn't solely be a child's; there should always be an adult present to check the guinea pig is getting the right care that he or she needs.

Another good reason for getting a guinea pig is that they are not generally destructive. Cavies are relatively well behaved and will not try to destroy everything in its path. However, you should always make sure your piggie is in a hazard-free zone.

Guinea pigs aren't expensive pets to keep. Most pet shops and garden centers sell them for around 20-30$. Cavies can get bored easily, so ideally, they should be kept in pairs or small groups, especially as they're herd animals. Of course, you can't just get a guinea piggie (or two) - your pet(s) will need a suitable home.

Hutches generally range from 50-200$ depending on the quality of the hutch. Cages tend to be cheaper, around 20-90$, although the price will depend on what sort of cage it is and what features it has. Guinea piggies will also need a food bowl, water bottle or bowl and toys to keep them entertained when you're away. Bedding can be bulk-bought or bought in small quantities. A large bag of hay generally costs around 7-15$.

Cavies will need food (and water). Dried foods can be bought in different quantities (a small-medium bag tends to cost around 10$). You will also need to have a constant supply of hay - for food and bedding.

You may also wish to buy sawdust (be careful though, as some guinea piggies are allergic to this material).

You could line the hutches with your old newspapers or magazines and put the bedding on top - remember to remove any staples first, though, and avoid colored prints as pigs sometimes chew up the papers.

Guinea pigs have great personalities, with each one being different. They also have a range of noises, mainly squeaks, which they use, along with their body language, to communicate to you and other guinea piggies.

Unlike the majority of hamsters, guinea pigs tend to have long life spans of about 5 to 10 years, so they are good 'stable' pets as they can generally be assumed to live for more than three years.

Again, unlike hamsters, cavies are diurnal; they don't sleep in the daytime and keep you awake at night. So, maybe the guinea pig is the perfect pet for you.

To learn more in-depth about Guinea pigs diet you can check our book called Guinea pigs Diet Plan for Beginners on Amazon.

NOTES

NOTES

Notes

NOTES

_____

_____

_____

_____

_____

_____

_____

_____

_____

Don't forget to share your experience
with us. It would mean a lot for me.
Thanks!